STUDIES IN VILLAGE INDIA

About the Editors

B.N. Yuganhar, graduated with first class Honours in Economics and obtained M.A. in Economics from Sri Venkateswara University, Tirupati. He taught Economics in the Madras and Sri Venkateswara University before joining the Indian Administrative Service in 1962. He worked as the District Magistrate of Srikakulam District during a period of historic turbulence in the district between 1969 and 1971. He was Special Assistant to the Deputy Chairman, Planning Commission from 1974 to 1978, and worked proximately with the national planning process and the formulation and implementation of the Fifth Five Year Plan. He was Commissioner, Special Employment Schemes; Chairman and Managing Director of A.P. Small Scale Industries Corporation; Secretary to the Chief Minister of Andhra Pradesh. He served the United Nations in 1981 and worked as consultant to UNIDO and was Regional Adviser, Industrial Development and Technology policies at ESCAP, Bangkok till 1986. On return he served as Secretary, Planning and Secretary, Industries and Commerce, Government of Andhra Pradesh during 1987 and 1988, before joining the Lal Bahadur Shastri National Academy of Administration, Mussoorie as its Director.

He has extensive experience in organization of training courses and participation in seminars and conferences in the planning, employment, industrial development and technology policies in India, Europe and Asia.

Neela Mukherjee, is currently working as Professor of Economics at Lal Bahadur Shastri National Academy of Administration, Government of India, Mussoorie (Uttar Pradesh). Her areas of specialisation relate to rural development and poverty alleviation on one hand and international economics on the other. She has pursued action research in selected villages of India on participatory approach to rural development and is currently engaged in documenting her experiences and observations. In the area of international economics she has worked on balance of payments adjustments of South-Asian countries at London School of Economics, London during 1985-86 on a British Commonwealth fellowship. As a senior fellow of Indian Council of Social Science Research she undertook research in the area of trade in services at Indian Statistical Institute, Calcutta during 1987-88. She has also been awarded the Fulbright Senior fellowship to pursue her research in trade in services at Stanford University, USA.

Dr. Mukherjee has a large number of papers on poverty alleviation, international trade and payments in both national and international journals and a few books to her credit.

STUDIES IN VILLAGE INDIA

Issues in Rurl Development

Edited by

B.N. Yugandhar

Neela Mukherjee

CONCEPT PUBLISHING COMPANY PVT. LTD.

NEW DELHI-110059

ISBN-13: 978-81-7022-361-0

First Published 2016

Published and Printed by

Concept
Since 1974

Concept Publishing Company Pvt. Ltd.
A/15-16, Commercial Block, Mohan Garden
New Delhi-110059 (India)
T: 25351460, 25351794, *F*: 091-11-25357109
E: publishing@conceptpub.com, W: www.conceptpub.com
Editorial Office: H-13, Bali Nagar, New Delhi-110 015, India.

Cataloging in Publication Data--Courtesy: D.K. Agencies (P) Ltd. <docinfo@dkagencies.com>

Studies in village India : issues in rural development / edited by B.N. Yugandhar, Neela Mukherjee.
pages cm
Reprint. Originally published: 1991.
Socioeconomic and political changes in the villages; a study.
Copyright: LBSNAA.
Includes bibliographical references and index.
ISBN 9788170223610

1. Rural development--India. 2. Villages--India. I. Yugandhar, B. N., 1937- editor. II. Mukherjee, Neela, editor. III. Lal Bahadur Shastry National Academy of Administration.

HN690.Z9C6 2016 DDC 307.14120954 23

TO
THE COUNTLESS VILLAGERS
IN CHAINS OF POVERTY
WHOSE
CHERISHED DREAM
OF A LIFE OF SELF-ESTEEM
AND
DIGNITY
WOULD SOMEDAY COME TRUE

PREFACE

The village study unit of the National Academy was started quite recently for deeper understanding and appreciation oi village economies, to strengthen training and research and publications in village issues. Village issues form an integral part of training programme of the Academy. One major part of training programme relates to village study in order to facilitate the officers to understand and appreciate rural ethos, the issues and the interventionist role of the State and other agencies in rural development. The Academy is a large storehouse of information on dynamics of villages emanating from reports of trainee-officers of Indian Civil Service from time to time. Within the short span of a year more than 200 villages are studied in different phases of training. This has generated a large basket of rich information and cross-section data on villages in India.

The village study unit has undertaken both spatial and temporal analysis of the village universe covered so far to see the socio-economic and political changes which the villages have experienced over the years. The unit pursues action research in important areas such as people-oriented development strategies and methodologies of people's participation and mobilisation, peasant movements and other related issues bearing on rural areas.

As a part of its action research and publication programme, the unit has initiated a series of publication on village study drawn from both the storehouse of the Academy and experts in the field. As a first step in this direction, the autumn issue of the journal administrator was published as a special issue on village study.

We place before you this edited book which is the second output of the unit and contains a collection of articles on different aspects of villages in India. We hope that the book will provide a fleeting glimpse of the multi-dimensional issues of village India.

Mussoorie:
20th December, 1990

B. N. YUGANDHAR
NEELA MUKHERJEE

CONTENTS

PART FOUR
SOME VILLAGE PROFILES

LIST OF CONTRIBUTORS

1. V.M. Rao
Professor and Head
Rural Economics Unit,
Institute for Social & Economic Change,
Nagarbhavi P.O.
Bangalore - 560072

2. Dr. (Mrs.) Neela Mukherjee
Professor of Economics,
Lal Bahadur Shastri National Academy
of Administration,
Mussoorie - 248179 (UP)

3. K.B. Saxena
Joint Secretary
(Land Reforms)
Ministry of Rural Development,
Shastri Bhavan
New Delhi - 110001

4. Nirmal Sengupta
Professor,
National Institute for Rural Development,
Hyderabad

5. Amitabh Joshi (IAS)
Assistant Collector & SDM
Nanded District
Nanded - 431001 (Maharashtra)

6. M.V. Rao (IAS)
   Assistant Collector
   Burdwan (W.B.)

7. K. Gopal Iyer
   Project Adviser,
   Land Reform Unit,
   Lal Bahadur Shastri National Academy
   of Administration,
   Mussoorie - 248179 (UP)

8. Rajat Modwel IAS (P)
   Lal Bahadur Shastri National Academy
   of Administatrion,
   Mussoorie - 248179 (UP)

9. Rahul Rasgotra IPS (P)
   Lal Bahadur Shastri National Academy
   of Administration,
   Mussoorie - 248179 (UP)

10. R.C.S. Bist
    Investigator, District Planning Unit
    Lal Bahadur Shastri National Academy
    of Administration,
    Mussoorie - 248179 (UP)

11. Amitabha Mukherjee
    Adviser, District Planning Unit
    Lal Bahadur Shastri National Academy
    of Administration,
    Mussoorie - 248179 (UP)

12. G.R. Meena, IAS (P)
    Deepak Agrawal, IAS (P), and
    Kamal Dayani, IAS (P)
    Lal Bahadur Shastri National Academy
    of Administration,
    Mussoorie - 248179 (UP)

13. Alkesh Sharma, IAS (P)
Tajender Singh Luthra, IPS (P), and
Anil K. Gupta, IFoS (P)
Lal Bahadur Shastri National Academy
of Administration,
Mussoorie - 248179 (UP)

14. Anirudh Tewari, IAS (P)
Manoj Ahuja, IAS (P)
Mukhmeet Singh, IAS (P), and
Charanjit Singh, IFoS (P)
Lal Bahadur Shastri National Academy
of Administration,
Mussoorie - 248179 (UP)

15. Rajesh Das, IPS (P)
Sanjukta Patnaik, IFoS (P), and
Trisaljit Kochar, IPoS (P)
Lal Bahadur Shastri National Academy
of Administration,
Mussoorie - 248179 (UP)

P stands for probationer
IAS stands for Indian Administrative Service
IPS stands for Indian Police Service
IFoS stands for Indian Forest Service
IPoS stands for Indian Postal Service

INTRODUCTION

NEELA MUKHERJEE

India has a mixed bag of experience in the development profile of villages. Each village has a distinct identity in the physical, socio-economic and political map of India in terms of its unique combination of material resources, human capital and socio-political ethos. The path to development of a village has not necessarily been of the 'Lewis' variety with structural shifts of surplus labour taking place from rural to urban sector or from agriculture to industry and thus contributing to rise in marginal productivity of labour. Neither has it necessarily evolved around the Gandhian path of 'village republic'. Over the years, each village has evolved its own pattern of development based on its societal relations, political milieu, economic opportunities and other resources. The development in most cases has been slow and not perceptible. The pace of transformation has also varied extensively from one village to the other. Yet, some transformation has taken place in the villages which have struggled to evolve their own patterns of resolving issues and inducing material progress.

The book contains a set of papers covering different aspects of Indian villages. The first part of the book deals with a framework of analysis and methodology for rural development. Rao in his paper focuses on the rôle of village studies in improving the planning process for rural development. After describing the recent advances in spatial-cum-sectoral approach to planning for integrated rural development, the paper emphasises the pressing need to anchor the approach to 'cluster of villages' and to take planning closer to rural people in order to integrate their priorities and preferences and to give them adequate opportunities to participate in the developmental process.

State intervention in villages has also been of a tall order in terms of a plethora of rural development programmes implemented at the village level. However, many of these programmes have staggered and have not yielded the warranted results. Several contending hypotheses have been offered to explain such under-performance. Some have explained it through shortage of funds while others have talked of deteriorating standards of performance caused by leakages and corruption prevailing in the system. Still others have pointed out flaws in conceptualisation of programmes and faults in their implementation. One major hypothesis offered is that our basic approach to rural areas or the top-down approach has been the top-most bottleneck for effective planning and implementation of rural development programmes. In effect, development programmes have been imposed from above without tailoring them to local expertise and talents available. Most of our resources in villages especially the human resources, their indigenous skills and expertise remain untapped. Participatory techniques such as RRA (Rapid Rural Appraisal) and PRA (Participatory Rural Appraisal) have emerged as an alternative to the survey techniques which have been traditionally used in planning for rural development, its implementation and monitoring. Of late, the importance of people's participation in rural development is being increasingly realised. The paper by Mukherjee is on participatory approach to rural development and related methodological issues.

The second part of the book is on a selected policy issue of organising the rural poor. The rural poor consists of economically and socially deprived sections of the society and are highly heterogeneous with regard to their economic activity and ways of life. However, the groups within the broad category of rural poor share common characteristics in matters of employment and exploitation. Saxena's paper deals with why and how of organising and mobilising rural poor for collective action. It is being increasingly accepted that active involvement and participation of rural poor in rural development can be facilitated only through such a process.

The third part of the book relates to socio-economic forces and political economy of rural development. Till now many of us knew that fragmentation and subdivision of holdings do not generally augment welfare. However, Sengupta has made an interesting study of how welfare of a village has increased as a result of fragmentation of land holdings. Coming to poverty alleviation programmes, the Special Component Plan (SCP) has scheduled caste and scheduled tribe families as its target groups. Joshi in his note has examined the degree of success achieved in implementation of SCP in Nanded taluka of

Maharashtra. Rao has made an interesting study of the political economy of poverty alleviation programmes in rural West Bengal. The political forces are as important as the socio-economic forces and need to be incorporated for realistic analysis of decision-making process in such programmes.

The last part of the book presents profiles of villages in Bihar, Himachal Pradesh, Manipur and Uttar Pradesh. The villages in Bihar relate to West Champaran district and are quite backward as far as socio-economic and physical infrastructure are concerned. Modwel has attempted to sketch a representative scenario of a village in the State of Himachal Pradesh on the basis of selected village reports. In the village profile of Manipur, four villages have been compared with regard to different aspects namely traditional economy, unemployment, demography and poverty alleviation programmes. Social customs and living styles in villages are many and diverse. Such customs and practices have been amply demonstrated in the study by Bisht and Mukherjee in villages of Jaunsar Babar in Dehradun district of Uttar Pradesh.

Amongst a plethora of village issues the book has focused on a few selected themes. Many important aspects of village life have therefore not been covered in this book. That in no way should undermine the importance of the issues involved in rural India which the book has not been able to touch upon. It is hoped that papers on several other issues pertaining to village India would be placed in future publications as and when they are ready for the same.

PART ONE

APPROACH TO VILLAGE STUDY AND PLANNING

1

ROLE OF VILLAGE STUDIES IN PLANNING FOR INTEGRATED RURAL DEVELOPMENT

V.M. RAO

The Indian economy has now reached the point where its performance would be increasingly judged by the results of development observable among the villages and the rural people, especially the rural poor. Reaching development to the rural areas is a slow and complex process. Even if the planning system is anxious to earmark substantial financial resources for rural development, many factors intervene to delay, distort and frustrate the development schemes. It is clear that the objective of integrated rural development needs the building up of an adequate system of planning at the district and block levels. While the weaknesses in rural development are often highlighted in terms of rural *vs.* urban contrasts, a point which turns up continually in the rural investigations undertaken in the Institute for Social and Economic Change (ISEC) is that there are marked intra-rural, and even intra-local-area, variations in development indicators. As an analytical response to this field situation, Rao had some years back put forward the concept of "cluster of villages" as the grass-roots level unit for planning and organising rural development programmes.[1] The purpose of this paper is to present a brief and indicative review of the evolution of recent thinking in India on the theme of micro-level planning with a view to bringing out the relevance and usefulness of this concept. Integrated rural development is a large multi-disciplinary theme and it should be admitted that the focus of this paper is on a relatively narrow and limited aspect of the theme. However, what the paper covers is a crucial component in the planning for rural development — a component which has still to receive the attention it deserves.

Spatial-cum-Sectoral Approach

Awareness that planning needs to be carried down to the district and lower levels has been a part of Indian thinking on planning since the beginning. It could hardly be otherwise considering the social and political processes preceding and leading to independence and it would be tedious to quote chapter and verse to illustrate an obvious point. However, concrete beginnings in this direction seem to be a much more recent phenomenon belonging to the period of late sixties and after. As a rough but helpful landmark, one can take the pilot research project in growth centres, sponsored by the Government of India in collaboration with 18 States and the Ford Foundation, as the dividing line between block level planning as a general idea and as a programme undertaken on a common and systematic basis in a large number of locations spread over the country. This project was initiated in 1969 and was implemented over a period of five years. Block plans were prepared for 20 blocks and, more important, an attempt was made to evolve a systematised and standardised methodology for block level planning. The central research cell of the project prepared a draft manual for block level planning which has been published by the Council for Social Development, New Delhi.[2] We take the concepts and ideas underlying the methodology described in this manual as typical of the current approaches to block level planning. It may be mentioned here that this methodology received endorsement from the working group on block level planning appointed by the Planning Commission in 1977.[3]

The manual bears a clear impress of the spatial-cum-regional planner's approach to rural development. Basic to this approach is the idea that the settlement pattern of towns and villages over an area like a taluk/block forms a hierarchy of 'service centres' of different orders and the core analytical task visualised by the approach is that of identifying the prevailing hierarchy by locating the 'high', 'intermediate' and 'lowest' order service centres and, in the light of this analysis, planning for extending a broad range of amenities, services and infrastructures to all the settlements in the block. This gives the 'general service centre plan' which is further worked upon by bringing together the sectoral scenarios — for agriculture, industry, education, health and transport — to get, finally, the 'integrated area development plan'. Taking up the concrete case of Talala block in Gujarat, the manual illustrates in detail and with admirable clarity the preparation of two plans. It shows that the Talala block, consisting of 49 settlements with a total population of about 70,000, has one 'high level centre' three 'intermediate level centres' and five 'lowest level centres'. Interestingly, the area served by the lowest level centre is seen to have a distance span of 4-6 kilometres covering 5 to 6 contiguous villages with a total population of about 8,000 — a grouping having close resemblance to the concept of 'cluster' of villages referred to above.

It seems obvious that the manual remains too pre-occupied with 'space' and 'sector' to look at 'village'. Once the hierarchy of settlements is delineated, 'village' retires from the scene and the criteria guiding analysis reflect chiefly the spatial-cum-sectoral aspect such as 'distance norms', 'population thresholds' and 'movement of people and commodities'. If one goes by the manual, insights obtained by analysing rural contrasts and by identifying the sources of uneven development across even neighbouring villages have no role to play in block level planning. On the other hand, the main burden of our findings is that, without such insights, planning for development cannot find its way at the grassroot level.

It is necessary to elaborate this point further by considering a premise which is crucial to the spatial-cum-sectoral perspective on rural development. This is the premise that balanced and even development can be achieved by building up 'growth centres' at key locations sufficiently high in the hierarchy of settlements. In the words of the manual, "we feel the term used in the pilot research project of 'growth centre', on account of the way in which economists use 'growth' and the use already made by geographers, should be reserved for places of a much higher order than what we will be normally dealing with in this manual". The premise stands out even more clearly in the report of the working group on block level planning. Distinguishing between the three types of activities requiring locational decisions — viz. (i) key projects in the productive sectors of the economy, (ii) basic infrastructure and provision of minimum needs, and (iii) setting up of grass-root level organisations such as co-operatives, the report observes "the first mentioned activity has a generative role and will be concentrated in a few specific locations which may be called 'rural growth centres'. The activities mentioned in (ii) and (iii) above will have a servicing role and will be dispersed in as many locations as necessary, so that they are accessible to the local population within a reasonable minimum distance. These will be 'rural service centres'.

It would seem that the growth centres identified by the spatial-cum-sectoral approach rarely descent below the level of taluk headquarters. The manual itself identifies only one 'high level' centre in the Talala block which is the headquarters place and the largest settlement in the block. A detailed integrated development plan for Malaprabha and Ghataprabha command areas in Karnataka prepared in the (ISEC) also identifies a small number of growth centres which are mostly the taluk headquarters.[4] As a logical consequence of the premise of 'high level' growth centres, the spatial-cum-sectoral approach assigns a relatively passive role to settlements at the lower and grass-root level. The main task at this level, from the manual's perspective, is adequate dispersal of a minimum package of services by identifying "the lowest level service centre and the villages within its ambit, which together form a viable unit which can support a minimum package of services".

Limitations of Spatial-cum-Sectoral Approach

It is doubtful whether this elegant hierarchical division placing growth impulses at the higher level in the hierarchy and provision of services at the lower level provides a workable model for planning rural development. It seems to us that underlying this hierarchical division is a mechanistic perception of space and sectors along with analytical criteria and norms rooted in such perception. The principal insight obtained in the ISEC studies is that the growth impulses need to be nurtured and built up at the level of clusters of villages in the words of the manual, the lowest level service centre and the villages within its ambit — and that the provision of a minimum package of services provides only the starting point in getting such clusters organised. The core tasks of rural development consist in fuller use of land and water resources, modernisation of farming, regeneration of village level non-agricultural and allied agriculture activities, building institutions like co-operatives and panchayats and improvement in health and education. All these are grass-root level activities requiring viable and compatible grouping of villages into clusters. It is indeed true that planning for rural development needs the broader perspective of a block or a district and, also, that certain categories of services, infrastructure, institutions and technical personnel need to be located at higher-than-cluster level. But the nature, quality and endurability of rural development achieved depend primarily on how well the clusters function.

The clustering of villages suggested by this line of reasoning refers to a much deeper issue in rural development than the issue of viable size of a settlement for a particular amenity or service. It refers to the subservience of villages to external decisions, their lack of capacity and initiative in organising development activities in their area of habitation and their inability to participate in — rather than only drift along with — processes of change and modernisation. It also refers to the tendency for villages to remain in relative isolation in even small neighbourhoods. Hence, the effectiveness of a cluster as a grass-root level unit depends not so much on the size alone of the population brought together but on the degree of integration among the constituent villages and social groups, quality of local leadership and capacity of rural institutions to bring the rural weak and poor within their folds. It is here that understanding the village as a community of people and as a part of a rural neighbourhood assumes importance in planning for development.

Need for a 'Village-based' Approach

Not surprisingly, this broader conception of cluster of villages remains outside the analytical reach of the spatial-cum-sectoral approach. At the same time, it is interesting to note that the approach does lead one to the point where the need for the broader conception becomes too obvious to be overlooked. A good illustration of this is the following observation made in a recent study on regional development planning. "In the case of India, the level that is missing almost everywhere is the one above that of the individual village, i.e., the small or medium sized town. It is the absence or structural weakness of this level which allows the centripetal forces to operate unhindered at the highest level — metropolitan centres — and to create towns which fail to generate developmental activities in their environment, leaving the country-side poverty-stricken and depressed, both economically and socially.[5] The mention of 'small or medium sized town' above the level of a village seems to reflect the spatial planner's reluctance to consider alternative ways — like clustering of villages — of building up the level above the individual village. It is encouraging to note that on this point the manual shows some readiness to depart from set ideas. Towards the end and in a concluding vein, the manual observes, "In fact it (demarcation of primary service centre area) begins a new entity — viable rural integrated service areas. The primary service centre and the villages in its service area, once the integrated packages of services start being delivered, become a cohesive unit for integrated development planning and administration." Thus, it is only at the limits of its reach that the spatial-cum-sectoral approach begins to get a glimpse of the rather new concept of cluster of villages sitting awkwardly in the conventional hierarchy of settlements delineated in spatial planning. It is not surprising that the manual stops only at recording its hopes about the 'new entity' without going into the question of rural factors and processes which might help or impede its emergence; clearly, these questions do not fall in the domain of spatial-cum-sectoral analysis.

Compared to the manual, the Report of the Working Group on block level planning considers more explicitly and fully the issues involved in mobilising and organising local people for rural development. Out of its nine substantive chapters, three are devoted to "institutional change and organisation of the poor". "Employment planning" and "institutional credit". The report observes at the outset that block level planning is to be viewed not as an isolated exercise but as a link in a hierarchy of levels from a cluster of villages below the block level to the district, regional and State levels. It is heartening to see the emphasis placed by the report on organising rural weak and poor, strengthening their status through employment and literacy programmes and institutional change and involving them actively in planning for development. While the report does not explicitly mention the concept of cluster of villages in describing these components of planning, it is obvious that they need village and groups of village-level organisations, institutions and programmes. In this sense, the report can be regarded as taking the idea of block level planning beyond the point reached by the manual to place it closer to villages.

The report of the Ashok Mehta Committee on Panchayati Raj institutions goes a step further.[6] Its principal recommendations for re-organisation will have the effect of bringing into being the mandal panchayat placed at the intermediate level between the village and the taluk. The committee suggests only one tier below the district level and the Mandal Panchayat, in effect, will be both a group of villages viewed as a single unit and a block reproduced on a small scale. The committee seems to feel that not only are villages, taken individually, incapable of serving as development units but, also, that the present blocks are unwieldy and large for grass-root level planning. In the structure envisaged by the committee, "The zilla parishad would be the first point of decentralisation and the basic unit of panchayati raj, endowed with a comprehensive range of developmental responsibilities. At the grass-roots level, the mandal panchayat will be the hub of developmental activity. Consequently, the block will cease to be the basic unit". Further, "A mandal panchayat would cover a population of 15,000 to 20,000 . . . balance between technological requirements and possibilities for meaningful participation by the people in development management can, in our view, be best achieved by grouping a number of villages to constitute mandal panchayats". Other supporting considerations mentioned by the committee include "economic viability . . . enable the people's representatives to exercise democratic supervision over the large number of micro-projects which are to be implemented at the local levels (and) are not entirely village-based . . . family-based programme, often covering as many as four hundred families, needs larger unit... would facilitate the forging of necessary linkages with the schemes for development of focal points and growth centres and would ensure efficient management of the growing rural-urban linkages".

Understandably, the committee is rather vague on how to delineate the group of villages and, equally, on the number of villages to be included in the group. The prototype it has in mind is that of a large "central" village with a population of 2000 or more and having 10 to 15 villages in its hinterland but the committee acknowledges the need to try other variants of grouping the villages. The committee makes an approving reference to the experiment undertaken in Punjab to begin with clusters of five villages each linked around a village built up as a "focal point".

We mention here two relevant points arising from the studies done in ISEC which should serve as a caution against looking at the cluster of villages only in terms of size.[7] The study on panchayats shows that the population size at which panchayats achieve financial viability is about 4000 covering 5 or 6 villages. But, more important, the power structure in panchayats is seen to be dominated by the rural rich so that financial viability by itself means little in terms of effective functioning of a panchayat as a development agency. The study also notes that the size norm for the mandal panchayat suggested by the Committee may turn out to be too large on the criterion of nurturing genuinely participatory decision-making and action by rural communities steeped in attitudes of passivity, subservience and relative isolation and driven by social hierarchy and strata. Secondly, the study on "planning unit areas" makes out an interesting and credible case for a two-tiered clustering of villages with the primary cluster of 3 or 4 villages serving as an unit area of development.

Planning for Rural Development — The Next Phase

It is important to realise that these ideas on clustering of villages are necessarily exploratory and tentative and will remain so until sufficient experience is gained in the field. They are significant, mainly, as indicators of the changing orientation of the perspective in India on block level planning. As we have tried to show, there is a shift in orientation as between the manual on block level planning based on the perspective belonging to the early seventies and the two later reports by the committees on block level planning and on panchayati raj institutions. This is the shift in the direction of focusing planning for development on rural people and villages without losing sight of space-cum-sector considerations; in this sense, the two reports build further on the foundation laid by the manual.

The critical next step in block level planning is to give operational content to the concept of cluster of villages. Getting clusters by relying on numerical norms alone will be about as sensible as trying to set up households by grouping together any five residents in a locality. A household is held together not by a fiat on optimum size but by mutual bonds of affection and needs among its members. While only a Gandhi may propose the household as a model for rural communities, it is nevertheless true that a cluster of villages needs strong internal links and bonds built up in the course of working for rural development which rewards all, particularly the weak and the poor. Planning for rural development needs the premise that rural communities are capable of generating and participating in a harmonious process of development. Not all social scientists grant this premise and, put boldly, the premise does look quite suspicious in the prevailing socio-political context in India. The planner at the micro-level will need to arm himself not only with a strong sense of commitment and optimism but also a keen perception of villages as communities of people; in fact, it is difficult to think of a planner succeeding in clustering villages unless he is also a practising social scientist. It is here that policy-making and research can converge to put to good use the social scientists' insights into villages and into the web of rural social and economic relations. Village studies occupy a prominent place in sociology and, more recently, have been gaining some ground in economics.[8]

Conclusion

Doubts are often expressed whether the villages are any more the distinctive social entities which they were in the past. The point is, whether the villages are distinctive entities are not, use of village as a unit of reckoning, observation and analysis is indispensable in block level planning, particularly in any kind of clustering of villages. Thus, planning for and by the villages constitutes the very heart of the planning for rural development in India. The present conceptual framework for block level planning, as we argue in this paper, consists of two unequal components. Therefore, on the one hand, a well-researched, elegant and articulate component covering the spatial and sectoral aspects; and, on the other, there is a set of preliminary and impressionistic ideas on the institutional and organisational devices — like clustering of villages — to stimulate active participation by all sections of rural people in the process of planning for and achieving rural development. The challenge of block level planning in India lies in the need to build up and strengthen the latter component and integrate it with spatial-cum-sectoral planning to place processes of rural development on sound and enduring foundations.

The problems in rural development which make it necessary to have "viable unit areas of development" have been recognised and posed as an issue for research and policy-making by Rao much before the reports of the committee on block level planning and on panchayati raj institutions. His comprehensive paper on issues and problems of development of Tumkur contains a helpful perspective for further research and investigation.[9] Of particular interest to the researcher would be the following observations which sum up well the rural scenario as seen from this perspective: "Rural society is not a homogeneous society. . . . Most Indian villages are dual societies, constituted by caste Hindus and the so-called Harijans, with a pluralistic addition of other communities and a confusing mixture of economic and power inequalities that sometimes cut across the divisions of caste and community. . . . Today, rural roads connect villages with towns rather than with one another. . . . There is a net emigration of skills and talents while imported skills and talents lack local commitment. . . . What is basic to integrated development that is area-bound is that the links among local resources, among local individuals and between them both are fully utilised. I must emphasise that I am not advocating rural autarchy or the splitting up of the country into a large number of self-sufficient and non-competitive rural markets. What I am advocating is the need for diversifying economic activity and allowing for the play of the multiplier effect in the unit areas of development, while at the same time allowing the facts of comparative advantage of resources and skills to link the rural with urban, State, national and international economies".

Given this grass-root level rural situation, how would one assess the prospects for integrated rural development ? The economists appear to be sharply divided in their assessment. While some believe that the job will be done once the government allots enough resources and adopts the right policies, there are others taking the stand that, in the prevailing political system, the intervention by the government could only intensify further the problems of rural inequity and poverty. The view that one gets in the field is that the truth is likely to lie somewhere in between these extreme positions. There could be little doubt that the planned development programmes are practically the only positive factor helping the rural poor and providing them a measure of relief but, at the moment, one cannot be too hopeful of these programmes developing the thrust required for poverty eradication. The closer these programmes are — spatially and in terms of accessibility — to the rural poor and the more their involvements in the programmes, the better will be their impact. It may also be expected that the development programmes, even of the relief type, would have side-effects favourable for the eventual politicisation and organisation of the rural poor. Thus, one can see the strategy for integrated rural development as an intervention with some potential to bring about desirable changes but it is difficult to be certain about the reach and dimensions of the resulting change. There are no easy solutions to these problems but, hopefully, the brief survey of recent thinking presented in this paper would be of some help to the planner in seeing the direction in which the integrated rural development planning needs to move.

As a preparatory step to the Eighth Five Year Plan, the Planning Commission has recently undertaken detailed exercises to formulate strategies, priorities and schemes for the 15 agro-climatic zones in which the country has been divided.[10] These zonal plans could be an important device to link up the national-level planning with the participatory planning at the grass-roots level. More important, the Eighth Plan approach paper has emphasised the urgent need to make the development strategy sharply more rural-cum-employment oriented.[11] It is to be hoped that this emerging new phase in the area of development planning would help in building up genuine participatory planing systems — involving villages and rural people — which have remained for long only at the stage of good intentions and oft-repeated slogans. Carefully planned village studies would be an essential intellectual input to guide the new phase and make it effective.

NOTES

1. "Some Neglected Factors in Integrated Rural Development", address delivered on the occasion of the convocation of Indian Agricultural Research Institute, New Delhi, 1977.
2. *Manual for Block Level Planning*, edited by Prodipto Roy and B.R. Patil, Macmillan Company of India, 1977. This manual gives a brief account of the pilot project, blocks covered, reports prepared etc.
3. See *Report of the Working Group on Block Level Planning*, (Government of India, Planning Commission, 1978), Chapter V.
4. *Integrated Development of Malaprabha and Ghataprabha Command Area*, B.K. Narayan, D. Vasudeva Rao, D.K. Narayana Rao, Institute for Social and Economic Change, Bangalore, 1977, p. 31.
5. *Regional Development Planning in India*, R.P. Mishra, K.V. Sundaram, V.L.S. Prakasa Rao, Vikas Publishing House, Delhi, p. 199, 1974.
6. *Report o the Committee on Panchayati Raj Institutions*, Ministry of Agriculture and Irrig tion, Government of India, New Delhi, August 1978.
7. These t o studies are *Panchayats and Rural Development* by D.V. Raghava Rao and *P.anning of Unit Areas for Integrated Rural Development — An Exercise* by M. Vivekananda. They form part of a series of studies done by the ISEC in the Tumkur district.
8. As an example of sociological village studies, see *India's Villages*, ed. M.N. Srinivas, Asia Publishing House, Bombay, 1977. Economic analysis of village-level data forms an important component of the Village Studies Programme (VSP) of the Institute of Development Studies, Sussex.
9. "Issues and Problems of Development of Tumkur", Key-note address prepared by Professor V.K.R.V. Rao for the APDI-ISEC Workshop on Population Planning and Area Development for South Asia held in Bangalore in November/December 1978.
10. *Agro-Climatic Regional Planning — An Overview*, Planning Commission, New Delhi, December 1989.
11. *Towards Social Transformation: Approach to the Eighth Five Year Plan*, Planning commission, New Delhi, May 1990.

[illegible]

[illegible]

[illegible]

[illegible]

2

AN ALTERNATIVE APPROACH TO RURAL DEVELOPMENT

NEELA MUKHERJEE

India has progressed a long way in the direction of planning and implementing rural development programmes and has gradually initiated successive improvements in designing of such programmes. It has been a process of 'learning by doing' in the absence of a structured model of poverty alleviation suited to the heterogeneous character of poverty which exists in India. However, the re-thinking and re-structuring of such plans and programmes have taken place with conspicuous lags and limited flexibility and the qualitative achievements from such programmes have remained far from satisfactory.

Top-down Approach

The rural development programmes have been conceptualised on the basis of an underlying philosophy of 'planning from above' or 'top-down' approach. Although the necessity of planning from and with the grass-root level has been widely appreciated and incorporation of some elements of 'bottom-up' approach have been attempted from time to time, the process of 'planning from below' has mainly remained at the conceptual level. As a result, planning for rural development has been on the basis of rural needs and priorities as perceived by the urban planners and it is their 'world-view' of development that has been administered at the grass-root level. Such views have not always matched with the needs and priorities of the rural poor which in turn have grossly undermined the effectiveness of such programmes.

The 'top-down approach' of planning is based on certain rationale which believes that plans should be conceptualised and formulated at the macro level and then flow downwards to the micro level. It is also based on an implicit assumption that the rural poor in the villages have limited capacity of thinking in terms of their well-being and hence planning for their upliftment has necessarily to be imposed from the top. In decisions taken from 'above' it also becomes easier to match the resources and the requirements of the rural poor from the top rather than from the bottom. The implicit rationale of such planning have been questioned time and again. The questioning has been not only in terms of conceptualisation and technicalities involved but also in terms of the results achieved through such planning process.

Supply-side Economics

As far as conceptualisation of 'top-down' approach is concerned it is based on supply-side economics. The stress is on the supply of goods and services to be provided by the State to the rural poor based on the demand patterns as perceived by the planners from ivory towers. There is little or no emphasis on the demand patterns of rural poor, the size of such demand and the involvement of them in determining the same. Practically no efforts are made to identify their priorities and demand patterns and to assess whether rural poor really desire the same basket of goods and services as planned for them from above. They are treated as mere objects in the developmental process and their involvement in decisions determining their own development is almost ruled out. The official delivery system as planned from top is virtually imposed on the poor households. This leads to a mismatch between demand and supply of goods and services which, in turn, often results in an inefficient planning process, failure stories, wastage of resources and ultimate rejection of the developmental process by the rural poor. It is not necessary to emphasise the obvious fact that the demand side of development is as important as the supply side and any approach not integrating the priorities and preferences of rural poor is bound to be stinted. The participation of rural poor and their involvement in the planning process in order to reflect the demand side of development would be a major departure from the conventional approach. It is also warranted under the present conditions where programmes for rural poor have failed quite miserably to keep pace with their expectations. However, such participatory planning is required to be based on a suitable process of people's participation for which a methodology is as essential as the approach.

Bottom-up Approach

As far as 'bottom-up' approach and the process of people's participation in rural development are concerned, one methodology has made rapid strides in recent years. A whole range of participatory techniques called Rapid/Relaxed Rural Appraisal (RRA)/Participatory Rural Appraisal(PRA) have evolved over the years which have proved to be very powerful methods for rural planning and appraisal. Such methods have already been introduced on a small scale in planning for rural development programmes in selected developing countries including India. The methods envisage a participatory approach to development. An approach where urban planners can learn from the villagers their knowledge, skill and preferences and in the process minimise their urban bias which go into rural development programmes. The techniques involve a process of rapport-building with the rural people and their participation in evolving plans and programmes for them.

The Assumptions

The RRA/PRA techniques as applied to rural development are based on certain assumptions which may be outlined as follows:

(i) The villagers are rational and aware of their well-being.

(ii) They are capable of participating and generating information to build up the requisite database for planning at the village level. They also have the necessary expertise in diverse areas for planning with indigenous resources, materials and technology.

(iii) Such information can be revealed together with appropriate insights provided the villagers are given an opportunity to express themselves and participate in the planning process.

(iv) The conventional methods of questionnaire-based survey is mechanical and fails to bring out many quantitative and qualitative aspects of village life. The large questionaire surveys have an inherent urban bias and the structured questionnaire for surveys is grossly limited in bringing out the perceptions, needs and aspirations of the villagers in a realistic manner.

The Techniques

A summary description of major RRA/PRA techniques is as given below. The major ones are participatory mapping and modelling, participatory transects, time line, participatory diagramming, ranking and scoring, wealth ranking and case studies. In participatory mapping and modelling, the villagers prepare the map/model of the village profile with chalks, colours and other materials either on ground or on paper. Such maps may be of dwellings in a village, of farms and fields, water collections, forests, soil etc. Participatory transects involve systematically walking with the villagers through an area discussing about different aspects of village life observed during the walk. It may relate to people, resources, soil, technology or any other area of village life. In the technique of time line, an historical account is given by the villager of how different aspects of village life have changed. Since it is difficult to remember the exact dates of important changes, the villager is facilitated to broadly connect the changes with major events, political regimes or a cluster of years. In participatory diagramming, the villagers prepare diagrams and charts (either with chalks or other materials) of various socio-economic and physical phenomena such as seasonal wages received, food consumed, prices , crops grown, rainfall patterns and others. The technique of ranking and scoring is applied to learn about the priorities, preferences and choices of villagers in matters of occupation, food, fuel, fodder, energy-use etc. In wealth ranking, the villagers map their households on the basis of their wealth. One can also conduct a case study where a villager can describe his household history, changes in occupational structure and other facets of village life and summarise major events and changes that have taken place during his life time. The use of different techniques mainly depends on the ways of expression which the villagers wish to adopt. The techniques aid in expression and participation. Much depends on the relevance of the issue and the way in which the villager wishes to present it and also his skills.

The Process

The techniques are for participatory planning and involve a process of rapport — building with the villagers. In fact, the information base of such techniques can be fully tapped and built only when a rapport is established with the villagers for whom rural development is being planned. The techniques not only help in knowing the rural poor and appreciating their perceptions, their needs and aspirations but also help in involving them in a participatory manner in planning and decision-making for betterment of their quality of life. From the observer's side, the techniques involve patience, understanding and an attitude to learn from the villagers. Some of the techniques may even require relatively more time before they can be applied because a process of rapport — building or warming up is essential in the application of the techniques.

The State-of-Art

The RRA/PRA techniques are still in the initial stage of development. Their experimentation and application have been in selected areas of rural life in selected countries. There is perhaps no upper limit to the whole range of techniques which can evolve in the process of involving rural masses. As pointed out by an ngo worker, the techniques are a language by which you enter into a dialogue with the rural masses. A language which both the villager and the information-seeker can understand and appreciate. A language through which an illiterate villager can communicate his needs and aspirations and participate in decision-making. It was amazing to build up time-series data from the responses of a illiterate Harijan villager, aged nearly 85 years in Ranga Reddy district of Andhra Pradesh who participated in construction of a historical transect or time line of wage rate and the standard of food representative of the poor in the village. The Harijan villager connected changes in the past years with major political regimes (under different leadership) and recounted the wages received and the kind and amount of food consumed. It was observed from the historical transect that although his wage rate had increased over the years from 6 paise a day in 1920 to Rs. 15 a day in 1990 his purchasing power had eroded drastically in the process which was reflected mainly in his consumption patterns. He observed that the process of impoverishment got accentuated in the decade of eighties. This re-emphasises the fact that inflationary growth has a deleterious impact on the standard of living of a poor household which generally has little or no bargaining power.

Issues to be Resolved

Since the RRA/PRA techniques are in their formative stage, many issues remain to be resolved in the use of such techniques. The data flowing from such techniques are basically qualitative indicating broad trends, description of issues and patterns of preferences and priorities in rural areas. Such data can be both related to a cross-section of a village or a time-series data relating to different years depending on the techniques used. However, much of the data cannot be quantified in precise terms. Hence, application of rigorous professional tools to such data may be quite limited. For instance, it may not be quite easy to build up indices on cost of living or apply regression and forecasting techniques to a set of data or build up a linear programming exercise on the same.

Information from RRA/PRA techniques reveal the perceptions of the villagers while information from the traditional techniques bring forth village-level databased on perceptions of investigators. Even when a questionnaire is designed by an organisation it is framed to elicit information on certain aspects of a subject which the organisation feels would present the real picture. Whereas, the other related issues on the subject which are important to the villagers are omitted because the organization is not able to perceive them from the villagers' viewpoint. In fact, realistic and informative questionnaires can be designed through group interactions based on RRA/PRA techniques.

In addition, data collected by both RRA/PRA techniques and conventional survey methods have their respective advantages. Hence, it is necessary to evolve a methodology for dovetailing the two sets of data collected to have the best combination of both the techniques. Such a methodology can help even for the purpose of matching data collected through RRA/PRA with the survey data. It is a question of combining qualitative and quantitative data for improving the information base at the village-level and action research in this area can help in evolving suitable methods for comparisons.

Further, since the present use of these techniques remain scattered and fragmented, the output from such techniques in the form of maps and charts are not located at one central place for purposes of collation, monitoring, research and publication. This task may be undertaken by a central agency sponsored by the government which can initially approach the NGOS (non-governmental organisation), different officials, researchers and others who have applied these techniques in selected villages. The agency can also plan for building up a wide database on villages using such techniques. It can also help in dissemination of RRA/PRA data which already exists and can plan future collection of data in such a manner that all villages are covered within a specific time span. There still remains the question of evolving a suitable methodology for integrating village-level data so as to present a macro-level picture of the issues emerging from the villages and for integrated rural development. Today, in the field of application of RRA/PRA, the village forms the primary unit on the basis of which the information is collected and built up. However, much remains to be done on the large-scale assembling of data involving several villages in different States for policy implications in terms of resource mobilisation and financial implications at higher levels. At the national or the State level, a macro picture of the villages can emerge only when the information received through RRA/PRA techniques is brought together and collated.

The Grand Storehouse

The villagers are a grand storehouse of collective wisdom as far as their own well-being is concerned. The storehouse remains virtually untapped. The villagers are themselves capable of building up socio-economic and even technical data on their villages and resolving intricate issues connected with their socio-economic betterment. This can be easily realised from the field-applications of a recent methodology called RRA/PRA techniques. The capabilities of the villagers need not be under-estimated. The attitudes of authorities have to change perceptibly in favour of learning from the villagers about the dynamics of rural development.

The potential of RRA/PRA techniques has been tested in bits and pieces in selected villages mainly by NGOs, researchers and some government officials and it may not be difficult to comprehend that these techniques given a wider canvass can emerge as far more innovative and exploratory than what the conventional techniques can actually offer. Many NGOs have started using these techniques widely in the field. It helps them not only to assess the demand patterns but also to establish rapport with the villagers for whom they work. It remains for the government to adopt them on a large scale for which some serious efforts are needed. Government can be a major facilitator for adoption of such techniques and also a user for its rural development programmes. RRA/PRA techniques have lately arrived on the scene of rural development and it is expected that major changes in approach to rural development can be brought about if these techniques are widely disseminated and applied in field situations. If they are promoted on a large scale by the government they can change the entire face of rural development programmes and their effectiveness in the coming years.

REFERENCES

Khon Kaen University, *Proceedings of the 1985 Internation Conference on Rapid Rural Appraisal*, Rural Systems Research and Farming Systems Research Projects for Khon Kaen University, Khon Kaen, Thailand, 1987

Jimmy Mascarenhas, *Participatory Mapping and Modelling — A Users Note*, Myrada, 1990.

Robert Chambers, *Rapid and Participatory Rural Appraisal — Notes on Practical Approaches and Methods*, Programme on Rapid and Participatory Rural Appraisal at the Administrative Staff College of India, Hyderabad, October 1990

Robert Chambers, *Rural Development Putting: the Last First*, Longman 1983.

International Institute For Environment and Development, *RRA notes*, various issues since 1988.

Hildebrand Peter, Combining Disciplines in Rapid Appraisal. the sondeó Approach, *Agricultural Administration*, Volume 8, No. 6, 1981.

PART TWO

PEOPLE-ORIENTED DEVELOPMENT

3

ORGANISING THE RURAL POOR

K. B. SAXENA

The number of persons below the poverty line at the beginning of the 7th Plan as per NSS estimates based on the 38th round (1983-84) was 271 millions of which 221.5 millions were in the rural areas. This figure now stands at 191.8 millions as per 43rd round (1987-88). The rural poor consist of economically and socially heterogeneous groups, such as tenants, sharecroppers, agricultural labourers, artisans, fishermen and other workmen in the unorganised sector of the economy. But they do not constitute an undifferentiated mass. Their income and social status are determined by their occupations. Though the rural poor are usually engaged in a number of diverse activities, for instance a landless agricultural labourer may also be a sharecropper, a tenant may also be an artisanal fisherman, these groups within broad category of the rural poor share common characteristics. These include a high degree of vulnerability to climatic changes, seasonal pattern of employment, low income participation, exclusion from many agrarian programmes, social exploitation through unwritten contracts which lead to economic deprivation and social degradation, insecurity in access to public services often due to lack of social discipline and proper orientation among local bureaucracies and powerlessness in the labour market etc. They are usually submissive to the elites in society and resign themselves to the so called 'fate' or divine dispensation. They are highly unorganised, lack the strength to bargain for their legitimate minimum and have low absorptive capacity and skills.

Development Programmes and the Poor

In post-independent India, the Union and State governments have introduced a number of social legislations dealing with the problems of social degradation, bonded labour, minimum wages, debt redemption.

land redistribution etc. Some special provisions have been made in favour of the scheduled castes (SCs) and scheduled tribes (STs) mainly in relation to reservation in government jobs. In recent years, a number of beneficiary-oriented poverty alleviation programmes such as IRDP (Integrated Rural Development Programme) and JRY Jawahar Rozgar Yojana have been launched which are specially designed to improve the income generating capacity of those below the poverty line. The widespread impression, however, is that benefits of these measures have not accrued to them to the desired extent. Many deficiencies have surfaced in the implementation of various development programmes and welfare services, some of which relate to leakages in official delivery system. This has been largely attributed to the lack of active involvement of these beneficiaries in the process of planning and implementation. It is in this context that the necessity for seeking their participation in programmes/measures launched for their benefit has been sought. This feeling has been increasingly strengthened over the years on account of the following factors:

— a trend towards 'tokenism' in implementation of development programmes with emphasis on statistical achievement rather than on substantive results, thereby affecting the credibility of the government;
— lack of concern for the poor in the implementing bureaucracy; their incapacity to enthuse the beneficiaries for seeking more active role in the programmes;
— inability of the government machinery to supervise and ensure proper functioning of the rural institutions like public health centres, schools, cooperatives, public distribution outlets, etc.;
— need for checking leakages and corrupt practices, the incidence of which is increasing;
— introducing social accountability in development programmes.

Panchayati Raj and the Rural Poor

Attempts have been made in the past to create a participatory mechanism in development programmes through panchayati raj structure. This has, however, not met with much success. The reason is that the rural community is not a homogeneous entity but is heterogeneous and differentiated. It does not seem possible in these circumstances that all sections of the community will be able to participate in its affairs at the same level of freedom and competence.

Disabilities of Rural Poor

The social conditioning of poor whose participation is being sought is essentially characterised by certain crippling disabilities which stand in the way of their active participation in the programmes. These persons are economically poor, assetless and are placed at lower rungs of society. In spite of their numerical strength, they are powerless and are subjected to social and political control by those who benefit from their weak positions. These persons also are generally unaware, largely illiterate and are lacking in ability to articulate their own problems, grievances and views. Because of these features, they are highly vulnerable to manipulation by more resourceful and powerful sections of society and are even made to work against their own interest. They are also amenable to divisive pulls which militates against their solidarity. Centuries of exploitations and dehumanising experiences have built a culture of social inferiority around them. The ideology of inferiority, submission and dependence has almost been internalised by these groups with the result that the self-reliance and creative self-engagement is not able to emerge and assert itself.

Reasons for Lack of Impact of Welfare Programmes

In short, the interventions, social, economic, legal in favour of the rural poor have not been able to make a dent on their depressed conditions on account of following reasons:

- Lack of awareness among the rural poor about their rights guaranteed under the laws and various development programmes introduced for their upliftment.
- Incorrect perception about forces which generate dependence, subordination, powerlessness of poor in society and aid the process of internalisation of this system.
- Inability to articulate their feelings and their concern due to fear, lack of confidence, isolation and apprehension of retaliation by powerful forces pitted against them.
- Extreme vulnerability to their manipulation by interest groups.

Inability of Rural Poor to Change Existing Conditions

Thus the rural poor are unable to realise their own potential to change their lives and the manner in which they should relate to the larger society. They also suffer from inability to alter their immediate environment to their advantage through group solidarity and action. Consequently they are unable to initiate programmes or change the contents of existing programmes to suit their interests and exercise control over those who administer programmes to ensure that benefits accrue to them.

External Impediments to Organising the Poor

However, the problems and constraints in organising the rural poor are not merely internal as listed above. There are certain external factors also which impede the growth of such organisations. These impediments are as follows.

Multi-interest Coverage

Usually the organisations which have taken up the cause of a section of rural poor e.g. agriculture labour have also lumped together various other demands of the peasantry. This has resulted in relegating the needs and demands of rural poor such as agricultural labourers and sharecroppers to a low priority. Those with affiliation to political parties work within a broader geographical and social set up and it is not at all unlikely for them to be influenced by the objectives of that broader set up. Such linkage often does injustice to local issues and problems. The leadership of many of such organisations has shown inability to identify issues which concern the rural poor and give them a viable plan of action to fight for it.

Legal and Administrative Set-up

The law and order administration is oriented towards maintenance of order and peace. The main burden of administrative procedures and traditions, criminal and civil laws, judicial pronouncements and practices is for the maintenance of *status quo* which means, in the practice, the maintenance and safeguarding of the existing property relationship in rural areas. Since the laws and traditions are heavily weighted in favour of the existing social order, the bureaucracy has developed a bias against any movement which aims at alteration of the existing social arrangements. The basic criminal laws also uphold inviability of private property as against other laws which tend to promote equity and justice. These laws are immediately invoked when any attempt is made to organise the poor to get their rights. The result is that the implementation of agrarian reform laws and other social legislations are short-circuited through provisions of Indian penal code or the criminal procedure code. The movement for just demands is perceived as a threat to peace and an assembly of men agitating for them are often described as rioters. Unlike the Industrial Disputes Act, 1926 which gives immunity to the office bearers of registered trade unions from civil suits and criminal liability in respect of labour disputes, no such protection is available in the agrarian sector where peasant organisations are not registered as trade unions. The inherent belief in the superiority of the law is so strong in the law and order machinery that in case of any apparent conflict between criminal laws and the land reform laws, the former is always given unquestioned precedence over the latter.

Economic Dependence

The rural poor, particularly sharecroppers and agricultural labourers have to depend heavily on the consumption and other loans given by the employer-cum-land-owner at exorbitant rates of interest. The situation creates perpetual indebtedness which has been well documented in various reports. Through this exploitative process, the rural poor not only lose their tiny bits of agricultural lands but also their control over labour power. Many of them end-up as bonded labourers, in this manner the rural poor lose their capacity to fight and, worse still, the will to live better. Further, due to the abundance of labour, the employers/land-owners play one-group against another thereby depressing the level of wages and extracting higher level of produce or work from them.

Social Backwardness

The rural society is also highly differentiated and hierarchical in which scheduled castes and scheduled tribes are placed at the lowest pedestal. If ownership of land and assets is taken into account, the landowners belonging to upper-castes are at the top of the ladder while the sharecroppers and agricultural workers from low castes and tribes are at the bottom. Because of a long tradition of social oppression it is difficult for persons belonging to these lower castes to organise and protest against dominant and upper castes.

FOR AWARENESS CREATION OF RURAL POOR

In this background, the need for creating awareness among the rural poor and mobilising them for collective action has been increasingly accepted as a pre-requisite for the success of welfare and development programmes. Legal interventions focusing on the poor on their active involvement and participation in these programmes can be facilitated only through this process. This has now been universally recognised not merely in various documents of national policies but those of international organisations such as ILO, FAO, etc.

Objectives of the Programmes

The programmes for organising the rural poor would have the following objectives:

- To change the attitude of the rural poor from passive acceptance of their existing reality to active self-determination and assertion.
- To identify their collective strength; enhance their self-image for building group cohesion and encouraging group action.
- To break social and psychological barriers which inhibit self-assertion and creative self-engagement; generating awareness in them about their own potential and power in protecting their legitimate interests and obtaining benefits accorded to them by various measures/programmes.
- To help them seek knowledge about matters concerning their interests, to enable them to demand programmes benefiting them and to revitalise structures around them.
- To organise them into a collective entity for exerting necessary pressure, articulating demands, voicing criticism and seeking a share in the process of decision-making about matters which concern them.
- To provide them wherewithal for economic independence and self-reliance.

- To equip them for exercising social control over development activities and for participation in the process of change.
- To function as a centre of countervailing power against the vested interests and their machinations for check-mating any attempts at subversion of programmes benefiting them.
- In case of women, to fight forces of gender oppression within as well as outside the family.
- To serve as a reference point for government for eliciting impact of its policies and programmes.

Advantages to Government

The programme of organising the rural poor would not only benefit the rural poor but would also have the following advantages to the government:

- With limited budgetary resources of the government, the programme would promote self help and better utilisation of the existing resources.
- The programme with urban bias can be transformed into relevant and more responsive ones for the rural poor.
- Organisations of rural poor would act as an intermediary channels of communication.
- Government departments are multi-functional. Organisations of rural poor will transcend these barriers and will articulate the interests of the rural poor.
- Improved quality of life will bring peace, social stability and improvement in economy.
- Organisations of rural poor can motivate field level functionaries in better performance of their duties.
- Organisations of rural poor can contribute to easing of pressures on government which is over-burdened with number of duties and tasks.

Not a New Idea

The idea of government through its bureaucracy entering into the arena of mobilising people and facilitating their organisation is by no means new. Some sporadic attempts have been made in the past in this direction by some agencies of the government which continue to operate at present. The earliest such attempt was by the National Labour Institute, a semi-autonomous organisation in the ministry of labour which organises rural labour camps in selected pockets of the country for creation of awareness among the rural poor followed up a process of facilitating their organisation. Independent of this arrangement, the Ministry of Labour has a Centrally-sponsored scheme for organisation of rural workers operating in 14 States/union territories (UTs) under which a honorary rural organiser is allocated a specially selected area. His task is to educate rural workers and motivate them to form their organisation. The Central Social Welfare Board of the Department of Women and Child Development of the Ministry of Welfare has also been running a programme to create awareness among rural and poor women. Camps for beneficiaries are organised under this scheme for exchange of experience and ideas and in the process developing an understanding of the social reality and ways of tackling their problems and fulfilling their needs. The Development of Women and Children in Rural Areas (DWCRA) programme which is an adjunct of IRDP administered by the Department of Rural Development also contains an input of organisation of beneficiaries as it specifically aims at formation of groups of rural poor women around a particular economic activity for delivery of benefits to them. The Integrated Child Development Scheme (ICDS) of the Ministry of Welfare also envisages extensive training to *anganwadi* workers who apart from providing certain services to poor women beneficiaries are also expected to promote group action among them. Council for Advancement of People's Action and Rural Technology (CAPART), of course, has a major scheme of organisation of beneficiaries for target groups of anti-poverty programmes to increase their awareness and strengthen their bargaining position. The scheme implemented through voluntary agencies involves training of animators and rural organisers and holding of awareness camps for beneficiaries. The department of education in the ministry of human resource development has also been implementing a scheme for training of social animators for revitalising the programme of functional and adult education. The department has recently initiated a schemes of *Mahila Samakhya* which aims at training of women in each selected village to function as activators and facilitators or *Sahayoginies* for organising the rural poor women. the National Literacy Mission in its programme of *Janshikshan Nilayams* also undertakes to train *preraks* who are expected to act as motivators for spread of literacy. The Government of Rajasthan has for sometime been running a special project of development of women under which they train village level workers called *sathin* and block level motivators called *pracheta* for mobilising rural women for social action.

Participative Content in the Existing Schemes

While the pattern in the above-mentioned schemes is on intervention from outside the government for educating the rural poor and helping them form their organisations, some development schemes of the government also envisage measures for seeking participation of beneficiaries/target groups/interest groups in programmes for realisation of its objectives. These measures include setting up of committees (informal or formal) with representatives from these groups, periodic meetings with the groups, dissemination of information to them about the programmes in a collective assemblage, creating informal organisations etc.

Major weaknesses of the existing schemes: The existing schemes for organising the rural poor or enlisting their cooperation suffer from the following major weaknesses:

> In view of the extreme disabilities from which rural poor and disadvantaged groups suffer, they cannot be helped to organise themselves by symbolic measures such as nominating them on committees, assigning them a formal position in any executive task or even efforts at consulting them on certain occasions. Objective conditions would have to be created in which they can be enabled to express their feelings without fear or favour and pick up courage to assert on matters which vitally affect them.
>
> Even in respect of schemes which aim dissemination of essential information about programmes among the rural poor and enlarging the area of awareness among them, the coverage is on such a small scale and is so highly localised in isolated pockets that there is no multiplier effect or visible impact on any substantial scale so as to serve as a model for replication.
>
> Wherever schemes for organising the rural poor have been implemented, the objectives have been diluted by the suspicion on the part of bureaucracy, inadequacy of the training input, lack of a long-term strategy and various operational difficulties. Even

conceptual clarity about objectives has been lacking in the implementing agencies.

The strategy for organising the rural poor has not taken note of the diversity of social situations in which the rural poor are placed. The schemes have, therefore, lacked package of measures to suit specific situations of a target group. Further, while an external input is necessary to break social and psychological barriers which inhibit the rural poor, this externality need not be provided in the shape/terms of an agency but could also be in terms of ideas, motivations, technique of communications and group interaction, confidence building and potential raising experiences etc. which have been missing from the package of measures.

Models of Organisations

From various programmes which are being administered for mobilising the rural poor, the following models emerge:

Awareness Generation Camps

The methodology involves organising a camp for selected beneficiaries for a period ranging from 5 to 10 days to enable them identify their felt needs and problems and agree upon a plan of action for raising their will power and promoting community leadership. About 30 to 40 participants are selected from a specified area who are subjected to community living and sharing of experience. They are also exposed to persons with experience and expertise on various aspects including government officials who come in contact with them in daily lives. Usually, by the time the camp activity concludes, a certain degree of solidarity is achieved which facilitates promotion of an organisation later. In some cases, a follow up camp is also organised to review the impact of earlier efforts in relation to its objectives and to undertake further supportive action.

Training of Organisers/Animators/Activists

This model envisages identification/selection of persons with some potential for leadership either through government sponsored agencies or voluntary organisations and, therefore, subjecting them to a structured training course in selected institutions where they acquire theoretical knowledge and inputs suitable to the functions they are expected to discharge. Occasionally, they are also exposed to live experience of organisational activity by attaching them to activist organisations.

Promoting Informal Leadership

This model does not envisage any structured process of selection of a potential organiser or an animator by an agency for assuming the leadership role. The strategy of mobilisation is woven around a process in which the target groups of rural poor are facilitated to frequently meet and raise their problems and thereby helped to throw up a potential leader. Once such a leader spontaneously emerges through common consent the training input is provided to him through informal experience sharing at various levels rather than through a structured and hierarchical information disseminating programme. The crux of the approach in this model is on spontaneous sharing and freedom of action to be pursued by the group.

Integrated Multi-level Awareness Creation

The distinctiveness of this approach lies in creating structure of informal organisations at more than one level facilitated by motivated and trained local leaders, providing an informal consultation system for spreading the social consciousness horizontally and thereby increasing the area of social solidarity and group action. Each level derives its strength from the other and contributes to the richness of experience sharing through which emerges commonality of problems and a programme of group action. This process is suitably aided by inputs from outside research/activist organisations and even government agencies. The impact of this strategy lies more in raising the general level of consciousness than in achieving specific gains on the issues taken up for group action.

Patterns of Organisation

In addition to the above models, the following patterns of mobilisation of rural poor are and have been in operation in various parts of the country:

In many well-knit ethnic groups, there are fairly active traditional community institutions, particularly in tribal communities, which discharge certain social functions. These organisations are generally not utilised for regulatory and development activities largely because their existence is not officially recognised and they also do not have a legal status. However, these traditional community structures wherever they are active and have a certain degree of vitality and dynamism can be effectively utilised for mobilisation of the rural poor and promoting their organisations with a suitable training input and external net-working.

Trade union is an old and a well recognised model for organisation of labour. Though this model has been largely used for organisation of industrial and organised labour, trade unions of unorganised labour also do exist. Most of the rural poor belong to an identifiable category of occupational group, each of which groups has certain interests to promote and common set of problems. They share a certain degree of commonalty around which they can be organised. Trade unions can be organised wherever such rural poor belonging to a specific occupational category are located. Though the existing structure of trade union organisation can be used without any difficulty, a simpler trade union bye law would need to be evolved for the rural poor.

The model of a registered society has been in operation on a large scale for bringing together people with common interests and pursuing activities concerning them. Most of the voluntary organisations/ agencies are, in fact, structured as registered societies. The structure of a registered society is relatively more flexible when compared to any other legally recognised organisation and permits far greater freedom of action and flexibility of operation to its members in pursuing their objectives than a cooperative society or a trade union. This model can be used in diverse social conditions whereas other forms of organisations are difficult to promote as their operational procedures are more rigorous.

An organisation of rural poor need not always take a highly structured form. It can also be a loose type of organisation — a kind of movement grown around certain common interests. The advantage of this kind of structure is that it permits the process of mobilisation more easily and quickly and can be effective and useful in certain situations. However, the disadvantage with this model is that in the absence of a structured organisation to succeed the movement, the gains registered in terms of enhanced social consciousness may soon evaporate. But the model can be effectively utilised for achieving quick results in the short-run in situations where the goals to be achieved are not obstructed by conflict of interests and social differentiation within its client groups.

Government, sponsored organisations which promote cohesion and interest articulation among specific target groups. Such organisations may take various forms ranging from setting up committees to other informal power sharing structures. But these organisations though lacking in legal sanction nonetheless help in the process of mobilisation or rural poor for achieving defined objectives and building up solidarity for specific group action.

Gram sabha as an assemblage of all adults in the village can be a very effective organisation in areas where the population of the village is more homogeneous and less socially differentiated and where the problems faced are commonly shared without any noticeable conflict of interest. This pattern of organisation is most conducive where the objective is to introduce social accountability in bureaucratic structures.

It is a structure with legal sanctity derived from the Cooperative Societies Act and has been widely used for building up organisations of specific categories of vocational groups around certain economic interests. But the cooperative structure has not been found generally suitable for providing illiterate rural poor an effective forum for articulation of their interests and promoting their solidarity. However, this model can be utilised in limited situations where its members have a fair degree of knowledge of its operational procedures and the objectives to be attained relate to the management of economic activities and do not impinge upon social action.

Some religious bodies promote organisations of their members for achieving specific social and economic objectives. For example, Catholic Christians in certain tribal areas have promoted thrift and credit societies for their members to cater to their credit needs to promote thrift and savings among them. In this model, usually, the management input is provided by the religious establishment and religious influence idioms is vigorously used for promoting group action.

Sometimes people face a common set of problems and spontaneously react in a concerted manner without any contrived external intervention. The sudden occurrence of some event triggers of group action. This pattern helps in bringing the concerned people together and in sharpening their consciousness. This model of organisation may sometimes graduate to a large movement later when their heightened consciousness on certain issues merges with larger movements espousing these causes. Chipko movement is an example of this type.

In certain situations, where responsibility is entrusted to a group of persons to manage a common resource equitably, this often takes the shape of a unique kind of organisation, which readies itself to accomplish this task by building up an informal but agreed method of resolving conflicts and ensuring realisation of its goals. The ready example is that of *pani panchayats* which are engaged in sorting out problems of water distribution within the village community.

When specific projects are funded by a foreign country or one sponsored by a foreign funding organisation/consortium, these are often implemented through the structure of an organisation centering around the project agency. The project agencies also undertake mobilisation of the people in the area of their operation for pursuing the objectives of the project and often create some type of organisations for this purpose. These organisations do not necessarily have a legal status but do permit interaction among its members and promote group action in activities connected with the project.

Organisations are sometimes built around a single individual or a group of individuals who either on their own initiative or under the influence of an activist agency outside take up the tasks of mobilisation of rural poor and promoting group action without becoming a part of that agency. The relationship between such an organisation and the outside agency is somewhat loose and without any formal linkage.

Some organisations of poor are built around the personality of a charismatic/dedicated individual. This model does not have a structure or a form but nonetheless promotes group action/behaviour through the influence/guidance/direction of an individual who inspires confidence among the concerned people. Quite often such experiments do get concerted into some type of formal organisation later when the area of activity expands or the following increases.

The Existing Programme of Organising the Rural Poor

The existing scheme of organising the rural poor administered by Council for Advancement of People's Action and Rural Technology (CAPART) envisages a strategy under which leadership potential within the target groups is identified and such persons are equipped with necessary skills and given other assistance which becomes instrumental in their spontaneous organisation and group action. This strategy is sought to be concretised with two streams of training programmes which CAPART permits voluntary organisations to take up. One stream of training is for persons amongst the rural poor who belong to the village and after acquiring necessary skills and confidence agree to work for mobilisation of their fellow-men for getting them the needed assistance under various development and regulatory programmes. The catalyst in this stream is known as an animator whose role is to inspire, facilitate and help the people in getting the requisite benefits. He also functions as a reference point for information and knowledge on programmes and policies which vitally concern rural poor. The second stream of training is for persons known as rural organisers whose goal is to help people form organisations of their own to achieve specific objectives they have in view. A rural organiser goes much beyond the stage envisaged for an animator in the tasks performed by him.

The animators are selected for their potential qualities of leadership, ability to communicate with and establish rapport with people, capability to influence and mobilise them and talent in handling and resolving local level conflict situations in a manner that does not hurt the interests of the rural poor. The selected person is expected to live in the village or the area of operation. No restrictions on age or education are prescribed. No official interference is permitted in selection procedure. The selection is made through a mechanism under which the target group members themselves decide who in their midst qualify for a leadership role. A minimum percentage is prescribed for women, scheduled caste and scheduled tribe population to be selected as bulk of the rural poor come from these categories of persons. The animators undergo a three weeks training in a suitable institution run by a voluntary organisation. The entire cost of training including board and lodging is met from the funds of the programme. The training curriculum focuses on information gathering, awareness building and conscientisation and skill formation. The animators after training go back to their village and start working on their own. The voluntary organisation responsible for their selection and training is expected to guide them in handling difficult situations. No remuneration is paid to these animators. Their work is seen as a natural culmination of their daily existence and interaction with outside world. The animator's area expected to disseminate to rural poor of the area information about schemes and programmes which concern them, help them articulate their view point before the authorities, create an urge in them for solidarity and group action, help them resolve conflict situations without outside intervention etc.

The functions of rural organiser are different from those performed by social animators. Their process of selection, training and support system are also different. The rural organisers are expected to take up awareness creation among target groups, building up confidence in them and enabling them to see their strength and weaknesses *vis-a-vis* other forces surrounding them helping them realise the need for organised and collective action and prevailing upon them to form an appropriate organisation for this purpose. The rural organiser is not expected to be a permanent feature of the area. After an organised or collective entity is formed and has started operating, he is expected to withdraw from the scene though he may continue to establish linkages and provide support system. The rural organiser is expected to shift to another area and repeat the same process. Since the qualities expected of a rural organiser are not easy to find in view of complex nature of functions to be discharged by them, persons with such potential are selected from awareness camps organised for the rural poor in areas affected by acute problems. In these camps 30-40 participants are brought together for a period of three to four days where they have informal experience sharing and learn basic information about programmes and policies, have interface with officials and are enabled to identify their problems and chalkout a programme of action. The camp strategy is based on a dialogic model designed to help participants reach the following successive stages:

(i) interest perception;
(ii) interest aggregation;
(iii) interest articulation;

(iv) organisation; and
(v) action.

During the camps, participants who display leadership qualities and interest in organisational work are identified for discharging the role of rural organisers. The process of selection is not a structured one but a dynamic process under which the potential is assessed through behaviour of the participants over a period of three to four days. No qualifications or age limit is prescribed. After selection, the rural organisers are sent for training for a period of eight weeks to an agency or institution that has wide experience in handling such programmes. The entire cost of the training including board and lodging is met from the programme funds. The training curriculum besides covering the features prescribed for social animators lays greater emphasis on equipping the trainees with ability to influence the target group for collective action and forming appropriate organisation. The skills in management of such organisation is also imparted.

The pattern of training prescribed for social animators is also adapted with suitable modifications for activating tribal community leaders. In several tribal pockets, tribal leaders command wide respect and are deep rooted in the social cultural ethos of tribal society despite the fact that established statutory institutions have over-shadowed them. These traditional tribal leaders, however have a great deal of potential for functioning as social animators in their area. The programme for training these community leaders is expected to help the process of checking disintegration of tribal community and to make traditional organisations dynamic institutions for serving tribal people. These tribal leaders can take up the work for prevention of alienation of tribal land, protection of tribals against harassment by non-tribals and helping them get benefits of their development programmes. These traditional tribal leaders can also play a vital role in protecting the interests of tribal migrant labourers, protecting tribal women against sexual harassment and in administering programme of small consumption credit for local needs. Unfortunately, however, under the programme of social animators, this specific stream of training has not been taken up on a substantial scale.

The above schematic pattern provides financial assistance for activities relating to training of social animators and rural organisers, training of trainers, holding of camps etc. However, if other models of organisation of rural poor discussed in this paper are also suitably incorporated within the structure of the scheme that is being envisaged now, financial assistance may have to be extended to individuals/agencies for other purposes also such as post-training assistance, office maintenance, legal support, periodical meetings, communication input, printing of literature, documentation, registration expenses etc. The existing schematic structure administered by CAPART would, therefore, need to be suitably revised. There should be nc difficulty is doing so once a decision is taken about the nature, scope and other parameters of the programme for organising the rural poor we have in view.

Issues for Decision

The major issue for decision is whether the task of organising the rural poor for attaining the objectives outlined in this note should be taken up as a government sponsored scheme. There is a school of thought which strongly articulates the view that the government is not an appropriate agency for promoting organisation of rural poor. Since such organisations are more likely to be critical of the government and may also get into confrontation with it in a large number of situations. The government bureaucracy is ill-equipped to perform this role sincerely and honestly. The experience has also shown that administrative machinery does not view favourably the assertiveness of rural poor promoted by non-official organisations. It has, however, been noted earlier in this paper that there is little evidence of non-governmental organisations (NGOs) mobilising rural poor on a large scale. Such activities are sporadic and confined to isolated pockets. In the circumstances, once the need for organising the poor is recognised, the task should be accomplished through diverse ways. The government should come out in a major way to take up this work through a well conceived programme in which the efforts at organising the rural poor should get financial assistance and social and political support. Such a programme would have the added advantage of removing suspicion in government towards agencies engaged in this work and bringing rural poor into the mainstream of national activities. The government itself be entrusted with the task of executing it. It would only imply that a broad conceptual framework would be laid down within which various agencies/individuals/institutions can take up this work receive financial assistance, technical help and political support from the government, wherever needed. It is, therefore, suggested that a central sector scheme for organising the rural poor should be promoted. The scheme may be funded entirely by the Central Government as the States are not likely to evince much interest in it.

Appropriate Model of Organisation

What model of organisation of rural poor should be promoted under such a programme? Various models, traditional as well as innovative have been discussed in this paper. There is a great deal of variety and diversity in methods adopted for creating awareness among poor, promoting organisation and pattern or organisations so created. It is neither necessary nor desirable to promote a specific model. Barring models or organisations promised by religious establishments which should be kept outside the purview of the scheme, sufficient flexibility should be permitted for different areas, target groups and situations to throw up appropriate organisations suited to their milieu and get support under this programme.

What should be the process of identification of rural poor for this programme? It would not be desirable to lay down a specific or rigid process of identification. Except where a government agency itself is executing a scheme of organising a specific target group of the rural poor, it should be left to the concerned agency which intends to execute the programme to decide on its own the process of identification within the parameters laid down for the scheme. Since the task of awareness creation and mobilisation of rural poor is largely undertaken by non-official organisations of different types, it may be desirable to evolve some guidelines in consultation with such non-official agencies engaged in implementation of the programme so that the process of identification inspires confidence of all concerned. It may also be necessary to specify that where rural poor are being identified for imparting training, a minimum number of such poor coming from disadvantaged sections such as scheduled castes, scheduled tribes and women should be necessarily selected as the bulk of the rural poor belong to these categories.

Thrust areas

While the work involved in organising the rural poor is enormous and the field vary widely, it would desirable to identify some thrust areas and specific target groups for priority attention. The following thrust areas are suggested below:

- areas prone to atrocities on scheduled castes and scheduled tribes;
- areas with high incidence of bonded labour and inter-state migrant labourers;
- areas of tribal concentration;
- areas of low wage levels;
- areas of acute atrocities/harassment on women;
- areas of acute poverty;
- areas of civil rights violations.

Some of the specific activities for which rural poor should be organised are given below:

- protection of scheduled castes, scheduled tribes and women against atrocities;
- implementation of land reforms;
- obtaining minimum wages;
- fighting against social oppression caste and communal bias;
- freedom from forced labour and rehabilitation of freed bonded labourers;
- income generating activities;
- obtaining access to the delivery system and facilities set up by the government for their development;
- obtaining credit and channellising savings;
- liberation from the clutches of the ubiquitous money-lenders;
- protecting traditional rights of tribals in respect of forest produce;
- obtaining justice from revenue courts/courts of civil and criminal jurisdiction;
- protecting their land from being acquired for unproductive projects;
- proper rehabilitation of displaced persons on acquisition of their land.

The above is not an exhaustive but only an illustrative list. The programme is intended to cover wider objectives than merely improving the reach of poverty alleviation programmes which the existing scheme implemented by CAPART seems to focus on.

Training

One of the biggest problems faced in the implementation of programmes for organising the rural poor taken up so far has been in respect of the training. This includes aspects such as competence of the institution, content and curricula of training, methodology of training, input support (training material), duration of training etc. The training programmes for organising the rural poor are a highly complex and multi-faceted task.

A structured training programme with focus on mere information dissemination through lectures by experts is not at all relevant to their needs. The training programmes for the rural poor should concentrate, primarily, on removing from their minds a sense of inferiority and feeling of dependence and subordination and helping them regaining their confidence. The strategy of training to achieve this objective would have to focus on experience sharing, participation in real life situations, ability to cope with stress and conflicts, capacity to carry together people with diverse interests, creative modes of expression etc. There are not many institutions/agencies equipped to carry out this type of training. The following steps would therefore seem necessary:

— to identify agencies, organisation, institutions, informal groups which have ability to transmit this type of training and have experience in this field in every State. CAPART may undertake this task with the help of non-official experts in this field.

— to design broadly curricula for training for different types of interest groups with sufficient social flexibility built into it so that various organisations and agencies can try out innovative methods. CAPART may mobilise an expert group consisting of individuals from organisations which have been doing this type of work and design such a curricula which need not have an element of finality. It should be subjected to continuing discussion and debate so that its appropriateness can be evaluated.

— to prepare relevant and appropriate training material/literature for the rural poor consistent with the objectives of the programme. This training material would have broadly two components, first, to provide general awareness and focus on group action and second, is orientation towards specific activities of particular groups of rural poor. The first component would be common for all categories of rural poor, the second would be different in case of each category of rural poor.

A large number of organisations/voluntary agencies have been producing such literature/material. This should be pooled and made available to training organisations/institutions. However, more efforts are needed in this area. CAPART should sponsor a programme and encourage such efforts.

Communication Strategy

The communication strategy is vital to the success of this programme. This would obviously be specific to the area and the groups being catered to. Each category and organisation would have to evolve its own strategy. However, the experience of various organisations engaged in this task should be pooled and documented for wider circulation and appreciation, CAPART should act as a nodal agency to carry out these tasks.

Support System

The programme for awareness creation among rural poor and promoting their organisation is a highly complex and daunting task, more so in the social and economic situation in which it would have to operate. The success of this programme would, therefore, depend upon the support system available to those engaged in the implementation of this programme. This support system would have the following components:

Financial support would be needed for the following:

— meeting the cost of training;
— training the trainers;
— organising groups activities of the rural poor;

Intellectual support for the programme would envisage:

— office maintenance and mobility of the organisation;
— communication;
— preparation and dissemination of training material;
— legal aid;

— pursuing specific economic activities;
— providing technical inputs and intellectual support to organisations;
— carrying out impact studies.

CAPART is already operating a scheme called organisation of beneficiaries under which some of these activities are supported by them financially. CAPART is engaged in the reviewing and rationalising the norms of financial assistance for these activities. This task should be accomplished in consultation with reputed voluntary organisations with long experience of handling this work. The revised norms of assistance may be applied to this scheme as well.

Intellectual Support

The programme would require a massive intellectual support from research organisations, voluntary agencies, intellectuals and activists, for preparing training material documentation and in the field of communication strategy etc. A large number of such organisations and individuals having abilities of this kind would have to be identified. CAPART should under take to accomplish this work on a country-wide basis.

Political Support

The basis objective of the programme is to awaken the rural poor and to make them assertive. Such a programme is not likely to be welcomed by the established power structures in rural society which stand to benefit from the present depressed conditions of the rural poor. They are likely to frustrate the objectives of the programme by creating law and order situations, generating group conflicts, implicating the poor in false cases, intimidating and assaulting the poor and resorting to other forms of retaliation on the rural poor. The beneficiaries of this programme may also be dubbed as naxalites or anti-nationals with a view to bring them down in the eyes of the government and its administration. Hostility and suspicion may be created against the organisations and agencies carrying out this work. It is, therefore, absolutely necessary that there is a clear and firm political commitment of the government, central as well as State, towards this programme. This commitment should be clearly reflected in giving necessary support and strength to the rural poor and their organisations against above-mentioned retaliatory measures.

Administrative Support

It has usually been seen that the law and order and development machinery at the lower levels do not take kindly to attempts at organising the rural poor because of the threats perceived by them to their existing position. The self-assertion of the rural poor would obviously dilute the authority structure of the bureaucracy. Attempts, may therefore, be made by them to stifle this process by various types of non-cooperative and obstructive activities. The administrative machinery may also in these circumstances become an easy instrument in the hands of the dominant sections and vested interests in rural society for unleashing repression on the rural poor. Therefore, along with a clear political commitment for the programme, reorientation of the attitudes of development of law and order would also be necessary in order that it may lend necessary support to such a programme. A close interface between the agencies organising the rural poor and the local administration would not merely be needed but would have to be suitably institutionalised.

Net Working

Most of the agencies organising the rural poor carry out this task in an isolated manner in a small area with little contact with and support from larger organisations or similar organisations working elsewhere. In such a situation, these organisations become easily vulnerable to various mechanisms of obstruction and subversion by the vested interests. They are also unable to inform the higher echelons of the government about the ground level realities and social dynamics of the process of change taking place in their area of operation. The result, often, is that the government at a higher level, solely relying upon the views of the local administrative functionaries or political heavy weights, takes a biased view of such organisations and acts in a manner prejudicial to the interests of the rural poor. It is, therefore, necessary that agencies/individuals engaged in such type of work are in contact with each other and together are able to provide support and sustenance and also are able to assert necessary pressure on authorities at appropriate level to protect the programme and the interests of the rural poor. The networking should also help in agencies/organisations taking help of the resource persons/technical inputs available with others. Therefore, networking among agencies/organisations engaged in this task would be a very valuable support for this programme.

Support of the Local Community

Any organisation/agency/individual working for the rural poor would do well to seek support for their programme from the local community wherever possible or at least from a section of it who agrees with the objectives of the programme or is not hostile to it. In fact, a conscious attempt should be made to cultivate this support from the local community because, in the ultimate analysis, support from even a section of the local community would provide much greater strength to the programme and the movement than any support from a political/bureaucratic hierarchy located far way from the area where programme is running. Besides, such a support would also frustrate the attempts of vested interests within the village as also outside it to paint a distorted picture of the programme with the intention of subverting it.

Continuing Communication

The programme is likely to be implemented in various parts of the country by small organisations working in isolated pockets. It would be absolutely essential to provide a forum in which they can periodically meet, exchange experience, learn from each other's successes and mistakes, share each other's infrastructure, technical and intellectual resources and suggest improvements to the programme. CAPART as the nodal agency for this programme should be able to provide such a forum. In fact, such a system already exists in CAPART.

Participatory Monitoring and Evaluation

The programme of this type should not be evaluated in a conventional way and through conventional methods of social science research. A system of evaluation in which the organisations engaged in implementing the programme as well as beneficiaries both participate along with other interested resource persons/research institutes should be institutionalised and this participatory forum should do the critical self appraisal. The benefits of such an appraisal should be made available to other organisations and eventually the lessons learnt from such appraisals should be discussed in the national level forum for continuing communication.

Agency for Implementation

At present, CAPART is nodal agency for implementing the scheme of organisation of beneficiaries of anti-poverty programmes. This scheme is entirely implemented by voluntary agencies. Financial assistance is provided by CAPART to these voluntary agencies in accordance with the financial norms laid-down by it. However, there is no scope under the existing scheme to assist an individual or a non-registered organisation or any other institution for this work. This is because CAPART is an apex institution for assisting the voluntary organisations only and its constitution does not permit to render assistance to any other body or individual. It is however, felt that the present scheme for organising the rural poor should not restrict the implementation agencies to voluntary organisations only. It has been earlier mentioned that there are various models and patterns of organising the poor and the proposed scheme should be able to provide assistance to individual/group/agency doing this work and seeking help within the parameters laid down for the scheme. But it is also desirable that CAPART should continue to function as a nodal agency for implementation of this scheme at the national level because of the flexibility in its administrative arrangements and the experience it has acquired in this field. It is also true that by and large the scheme is likely to be implemented by voluntary organisations only. If the pattern suggested in this paper for assisting those engaged in organising the rural poor is accepted, CAPART would have to be suitably authorised to provide assistance to non-voluntary organisations also.

Financial Provision for the Scheme

A meagre allocation was made for this scheme of organisation of beneficiaries in the budget of the CAPART during the initial years 1985-86 to 1988-89. The total allocations during the four years merely aggregated to Rs.3.25 crores. However, the scheme was considerably enlarged in scope and size and EFC approved the extension of the scheme and agreed to an outlay of Rs.17.95 crores for remaining two years of the Seventh Plan. It has not been possible for CAPART to release the entire amount allocated for this scheme because of the paucity of suitable voluntary organisations to take up this work. However, the suggested pattern of the scheme which seeks to further enlarge its scope and range of assistance would no doubt require much higher level of allocations in order that the tempo of the programme can be sustained and progressively increased during the Eighth Plan. It is, therefore, suggested that a minimum of Rs.50 crores should be earmarked for this programme during the Eighth Plan. In fact, the suggested allocation is quite conservative considering the fact that on an average, Rs.10 crores were allocated for each of the two years of the last plan itself. It would not be desirable to have too ambitious a programme at this stage which may be beyond the capacity of CAPART to administer and implementing agencies to absorb. There should however be revision of the allocation if the existing allocations are exhausted and satisfactory feedback is available about the impact of the scheme.

Integration with Other Schemes

It has been mentioned in earlier part of this note that there are various schemes of organising the rural poor which are currently under operation in different departments/ministries of the government. The basic objective of these schemes is essentially the same i.e., to create awareness in the rural poor and help them in getting the benefit of various development programmes. Although each scheme administered by a department/ministry may be focusing the efforts to achieve the specific programme objectives rather than on general awareness encompassing various other matters which affect the lives of the rural poor, it does, however, seem necessary that in any area where a scheme for organising the rural poor is under operation, irrespective of the department/ministry handling it, it should integrate with similar schemes of other departments so that there is no duplication in effort and overall impact of the programme is better. Besides, the life of a rural poor cannot be perceived as fragmented into various compartments. Therefore, if the general consciousness of the rural poor about various matters concerning him improves, it is likely to result in more satisfactory implementation of development programmes and accrual of benefits for them. In the circumstances, separate awareness creation programmes for different departmental activities would no longer be necessary. It may also be provided that in any area where the scheme of organising the rural poor of a particular government department/agency or even a non-official organisation is being implemented that area may be excluded from the coverage under the programme proposed in this paper and the programme already being run should be made more broad based to cover a wider set of objectives. The basic idea is to avoid too many schemes and agencies operating in the same area for achieving the same objective. Also, a scheme of organising the rural poor for achieving the objectives of a departmental programme should also aim at improving the general consciousness of the rural poor as well. To facilitate this linkage, CAPART should be declared as a nodal agency for all programmes which have a component of awareness creation and organising the rural poor.

A Simpler Legal Structure

The need for evolving an appropriate legal structure and framework for organisations of rural poor and weaker sections has received virtually no attention so far. The trade union, co-operative society and registered society are the three legal structures in operation at present. However, the rural poor have difficulties in effectively participating within the framework of all these three systems. It is recognised that as the process of organising the rural poor makes headway, those involved in it would feel the necessity to convert themselves into a formal organisation with a view to assert their collective identity more sharply, get protection of the law and benefit of some developmental programmes. In view of this, one may consider evolving a simpler pattern of organisational structure with legal sanctity different from the existing ones in which rural poor (mostly illiterates) can operate with ease, legal procedures are within their range of comprehension and there is less scope for interventions/manipulations from above or outside. The department of rural development may constitute a small group to work out in consultation with ministry of law, the legal structure of such an organisational model.

PART THREE

A SPECTRUM OF VILLAGE ISSUES

4

SPATIAL DISTRIBUTION OF LANDHOLDINGS

NIRMAL SENGUPTA

Village studies may reveal surprising phenomena, as this one. This is a story of a village I studied in the early eighties. The village received its water from a diversion channel which served a few thousand hectares in several villages. These channels, locally called *pynes*, are very old, may be a thousand years or more. They constitute the traditional *ahar-pyne* irrigation system of Bihar, which are indeed, nothing but the so-called 'tanks of south India'.[1] The villages had a tank which stored water from the diversion channel. The stored water used to be drawn out through three outlets and, through supply channels were led into three different ayacuts irrigating about a thousand hectares. Two of these ayacuts were located within the village boundary, the third one was in an adjacent village. Here I will describe the management of irrigation in one of these two ayacuts.

Management of Irrigation

This particular ayacut was nearest to the diversion channel. It was the smallest one and had a command area approximately 40 hectares. Of these, about three hectares were made of irrigation ditches, unirrigable uplands and water-logged lowlands. Altogether 34.2 hectares were utilised for irrigated kharif crop. The whole ayacut consisted of 351 plots and were owned by 36 households. The top-most landholding size in the ayacut however, was 5.3 hectares. Thus the distribution of land within the ayacut was highly uneven. Indeed, concentration of landholding was acute also on the wider canvass. The biggest landowner had, not only 5.3 hectares in the ayacut, but more than 50 hectares of holding in the village and outside. Of this, a substantial part was irrigated and double-cropped. On the other extreme, several of the small landowners of the ayacut were poor and marginal farmers going by their total landholdings. Obviously, the landholding pattern in the village too, was highly uneven. Yet, the bigger landlords did not monopolise the whole of the irrigation water as it would be expected in this case. This happened because of the characteristic fragmentation of holdings.

Landholding Patterns

Table shows 4.1 the landholdings patterns of the households in the ayacut. Since plots do not necessarily correspond to separate fragments we have also shown the parcels. A parcel has been defined by the National Sample Survey organisation as "all land surrounded by land of other holdings or by land not forming part of any holding". The 351 plots aggregated to 152 parcels.

TABLE 4.1: Distribution of landholdings in the Ayacut

Sl. No.	Fractile group	Average number of plots	Average area of plot parcels	Average number of owned (ha.)	Total area
(1)	(2)	(3)	(4)	(5)	(6)
1.	Top 10 households	21.1	0.1016	6.9	22.4
2.	Middle 10 households	9.3	0.084	4.6	7.8
3.	Lowest 16 households	2.9	0.087	2.3	4.1
	Total 36 households	9.7	0.097	4.2	34.2

The distribution of these parcels followed an interesting pattern. Except in rare instances, the parcels belonging to any particular household was widely scattered all over the ayacut. In effect, almost all the landowners were interested in getting all parts of the ayacut irrigated properly. This helped in avoidance of tail-end syndrome found frequently in irrigation systems, where the farmers at the head-reach take away disproportionate share of water.

Even though it appears to be a strange phenomenon, indeed, it is not so. Let us imagine the condition of the land market in the villages. It is certainly an imperfect market. In the past, at any particular time only some fragments of land in the ayacut were available for transaction, since peasant-farmers do not easily part with their holdings. Any purchaser therefore, had only a limited choice of plots at a given time. The number of potential purchasers too might have been limited, and it was further restricted if considerations like kinship or friendliness entered into the transactions. Even though only the handful of big landowners were the purchasers, the availability of land, in a coercion-free situation, might not have any relation with the locations of the rest of the holdings.[2]

Contribution of Additional Factors

There were some additional factors which also contributed to the equitable (proportionate) distribution and good management. Except one, all the landowners of that ayacut resided in a single *tola* (hamlet) of that village. This helped in easy communication. Indeed, there was no conscious effort to make this type of residential arrangement. All those who had ever owned land in this ayacut but were not residents of the same hamlet, had not received any formal information about the date of irrigation. Some of them thereafter, decided to shift their residences to this hamlet; the rest had sold off their holdings. The landowners belonged to many different castes, although one dominated.

In a normal year when the tank was full, it retained water for about three weeks. If there was no rainfall during the period then the farmers were totally dependent on the tank water for irrigation. This area has an average annual rainfall below 1000 mm along with high irregularity. Therefore, spells of rainless days are not uncommon. In one of the years, during the study I found that with every passing rainless day, the villagers' worries were increased. Finally, a group decided to release the tank water. They met the hamlet leader for his approval. Once he agreed the news was quickly circulated throughout the hamlet that the sluices would be opened next day. It was opened in the next morning. Until the end of the ayacut was irrigated most of the people attended. They had to, because many of them had some parcels towards the tail. Once every plot was properly irrigated the sluice was closed. This happened very smoothly.

Some Reflections on Fragmentation

In most of the south Indian tanks cultivation of tank beds is prohibited by government order. Many of these used to be cultivated even till the fifties. In Bihar, the practice still continues in many villages, as in this case. The reason why tank-bed cultivation was declared illegal was that, in course of time, the farmers did not wish their fields to get water-logged. In the village in Bihar this too was prevented by fragmentation of holdings. There was an unwritten understanding that a farmer having no land in any of the three ayacuts irrigated from the tank should not own any land in the tank bed. Not only that, it was also implied that every such landowner should have more landholding in the ayacut than in the tank bed so that their interest in using the bed primarily as tank remained as the dominant interest. In that area land consolidation operation was going on. The villagers did impress on the officials not to consolidate landholdings within the tank bed and in the ayacuts, and to retain these two in proportion 1: 2 at least. Thus, except for the very deep parts near the main embankments nearly three-fourths of the tank bed was cultivated. During the kharif season they raised a water-resistant long variety of paddy with nominal yield. But during the rabi season, when the tank bed contained excellent subsoil moisture, they reaped a very good harvest of cash crops. For this purpose, after the kharif season, during Dussehera, the tank used to be emptied in a ceremonial manner.

This is not an unusual phenomenon. I had come across this kind of fragmentation while conducting studies in other parts of Bihar and once in a while, also in South India. The very high degree of fragmentation noted in this village was not so widely prevalent. But still, the distributive effect was the same. The areas were generally the ones where there were traditional irrigation systems, which would require a lot of groupwork for maintenance of the physical structures. The equitable (proportionate) distribution ensured that everyone, big or small holder, were interested in the proper maintenance of the irrigation system. If this is the reason it is also likely that similar phenomenon were present in common property management other than irrigation. Here we have explained now the process occurred without any conscious monitoring. This shows, that such distribution may exist even under imperfect market conditions, without much effort. It may be recalled however, that in past, in Indian villages, landholdings used to be redistributed from time to time. But the norms and procedures in such redistribution are not known. Therefore, one cannot be certain that the purpose was to meet this demand of communal tasks or the norms were the same as observed here.

Fragmentation of landholdings is a phenomenon which was once widely prevalent all over the world. Its persistence is also well-recorded. There is but little difference among the development experts that consolidated holdings are far superior to fragmented ones. It is generally believed that fragmentation was a consequence of division of property through inheritance. But this seems to be only partly true. Many scholars have pointed out that the phenomenon was not without its rationale.[3] The present study goes in support of that, and shows that the fragmentation did help immensely in equitable distribution of irrigation benefits and good management of the resource in question.

NOTES

1. Sengupta, N. : "Indigenous Irrigation and Social Organisation in South Bihar" *Indian Economic and Social History Review*, 22(2), 1980.
2. Essentially, the situation in the long-run may be hypothesised as selection of 'n' independent fragments by a landowner from all the fragments in the ayacut, where 'n' stands for the number of parcels owned by the person. Unfortunately, the theoretical distributions cannot be worked out when the fragments are of different sizes and the number of parcels owned by a landowner vary. This deprives us of a statistical test to verify whether the actual distribution we found agrees with the hypothesis. But an approximate test may be designed. From the central limit theorem one knows, that if the selection process made by a farmer is independent of locational characteristic, the locational mean of all the fragments belonging to him will be at the locational mean of the total land in the ayacut, and the variance of the sample mean will decrease as 'n', the number of parcels, increase. In the case study, the variance of mean locations of the landholdings of each landholder in the ayacut is only 24 per cent of the variance for plot locations in the ayacut.
3. (i) Bray, F.A.: *The Rice Economies : Technology and Development in Asian Societies*, Oxford, Basil Blackwell, 1986;
   (ii) Dahlman, Carl J. : *Open Field System and Beyond. A Property Right Analysis of an Economic Institution*, Cambridge, Cambridge University Press, 1980;
   (iii) Fenoaltea, S.: "Risk, Transaction Cost and the Organization of Medieval Agriculture", *Explorations in Economic History*, No. 13, 1976;
   (iv) Heston, Alan and Kumar, Dharma : "The Persistence of Land Fragmentation in Peasant Agriculture: An Analysis of South Asian Cases", *Explorations in Economic History*, No. 20, 1983;
   (v) McCloskey, D.N. : "The Persistence of English Common Fields" and "The Economics of Enclosures : A Market Analysis", in W.N. Parker and E.L. Jones (ed.) *European Peasants and Their Markets*. Princeton, Princeton University Press, 1975.

5

A NOTE ON SPECIAL COMPONENT PLAN IN NANDED TALUKA OF MAHARASHTRA

AMITABH JOSHI

Special component plan (SCP) is especially targeted towards helping the scheduled caste and scheduled tribe families living below the poverty line in order to enable them to cross it. This is sought to be achieved through provision of income generating assets and creation of self-employment ventures. The target group families are provided with a package of assistance including institutional credit and subsidy support. The selection of households are on the basis of certain norms. Scheduled caste (SC) and scheduled tribe (ST) families, listed in 'below poverty line' (BPL) list, and satisfying the following two criteria, namely, having agricultural land less than six hectares and annual family income of less than Rs.4,800 are selected for assistance under the SCP Programme.

Nature of Schemes under the Programme

Special Component Plan (SCP) as implemented by *panchayat samiti* office and *zilla parishad*, is basically a programme dealing with primary sector schemes. The four major primary sector schemes (agriculture and allied activities) implemented by *panchayat samiti* office may be grouped as follows:

- land development schemes which includes schemes for soil and water conservation, *nulla* bunding, increasing the productivity of soil and others;
- minor irrigation schemes;
- schemes for provision of agricultural inputs such as spray pumps,

seeds and fertilizers;
- bullock pair and bullock-cart schemes.

The subsidy limits fixed for the above-mentioned four schemes vary from one group of schemes to the other. In land development there is a 10 per cent subsidy up to a financial loan limit of Rs.4,500. The agricultural input scheme has a 100 per cent subsidy up to a loan limit of Rs.2,150. In minor irrigation there is 50 per cent subsidy up to a loan limit of Rs.9,000 whereas, for a bullock-cart and a bullock pair it is a 50 per cent subsidy up to a loan limit of Rs.3,000. A beneficiary can avail of more than one scheme. In fact in Nanded taluka, all the 70 identified beneficiaries have availed of more than one scheme. The beneficiary can avail more than one scheme under SCP within a subsidy limit of Rs.9,650. The beneficiary is sought to be assisted over a period of three to four years during which incremental inputs of financial support are provided in a phased manner. For Nanded taluka, 70 beneficiaries were identified for assistance under SCP. There is a full-fledged section in the office of the BDO (Block Development Officer) which deals exclusively with SCP.

The present study aims at observing the implementational efficacy of the programme and its achievements if any. For this purpose,villages and beneficiaries were selected at random. The villages were as follows:

- Barad village (a major village in terms of social, economic and political activity with a population size above 5000);
- Shambholi (a small village);
- Patnoor village (a small village with a heavy concentration of SC/ST families);
- Ardhapur village (another village with a mixed population of more than 5000 people);
- Sugaon village (a small village);
- Moghat village (a small village).

The field methodology was based on interview of the beneficiaries and visual evaluation and verification of the scheme's efficacy.

Some Findings

The major findings of the survey on SCP implementation in Nanded taluka are as follows:

Due to smallness of size of beneficiaries (only 70 identified beneficiaries) the intensity of the focus of SCP is quite sharp. The 'size' factor had made for a definite advantage for efficacy of SCP unlike some other programme implemented on a larger scale. It was not very difficult to observe during the survey that SCP unlike IRDP (Integrated Rural Development Programme), was able to deliver the goods to a considerable extent. All the four major groups of schemes under SCP were functioning quite effectively, and the monitoring and follow-up measures were quite prompt and satisfactory.

One may observe on the basis of the survey that by and large, from implementation point of view, SCP has performed relatively better than other anti-poverty programmes in Nanded taluka. It has contributed perceptibly in raising the annual income of the target group, and improving their quality of life. The socio-economic standards have gone up in case of nearly 80 per cent to 90 per cent of beneficiaries. A mere 10 per cent to 15 per cent of beneficiaries have not been able to avail the opportunity to a perceptible extent because of local factors such as poor soil conditions, failure of crops due to natural forces such as floods, hailstorm etc. and inefficient utilisation of agricultural inputs such as seeds and fertilizers.

The reasons for the success of the programme may be summarised as follows:

The small size of beneficiaries (only seventy identified beneficiaries in Nanded taluka) makes for better handling. The focus can be intensified due to a manageable number of beneficiaries under SCP. With one section exclusively looking after 70 identified beneficiaries, there is timely monitoring and follow up of each beneficiary's performance. Also the requisite technical expertise being available with the BDO office, the schemes have lower probability of under-performing due to lack of necessary technical support and guidance.

The provision to avail benefits of more than one scheme simultaneously has many plus points. For e.g. a beneficiary can simultaneously avail of all the four schemes, i.e. soil improvement, minor irrigation, agricultural inputs, and bullock pair/cart scheme. As a result, these schemes which are generally complementary in nature, have cumulatively benefited the farmer beneficiary.

The loan and subsidy support limit is also quite high where total subsidy limit is Rs.9,650. Besides this financial support is given on an incremental basis annually over a period of 3-4 years. As a result, the productive assets are given time to 'concretise' and bear fruits. The banking circles also were less sceptical about advancing loan and subsidy support to SCP beneficiaries, perhaps due to the relative success of the programme. However, one did discern a universal hesitation on part of bank officials, towards advancing of credit support to rural sector in general, and the weaker sections in particular. This was due to the unsatisfactory performance of rural sector-oriented schemes and the absence of quick and profitable returns on these schemes. However, record of loan repayment was better in case of SCP than that of IRDP.

The complaints of the beneficiaries were more directed against the harassment done by the district land record registration office in evaluation of their land value. However, as far as complaints against the prime implementing agency for the programme, namely the office of BDO is concerned there were none. Instead, one could observe a rapport and understanding between the implementing staff and the beneficiary, with both the parties making efforts to contribute to the success of the programme. One may be justified in mentioning the commendable role of the agricultural extension officer and the junior engineer, responsible for implementation of the programme in BDO office. Both were found dedicated, hard working and sincere officials having a good understanding of the field conditions and of beneficiary's perceptions and aspirations. Their leadership did make a difference in effective implementation of SCP.

6

POLITICAL INTERVENTION AND POVERTY ALLEVIATION PROGRAMMES

M. V. RAO

India like any other developing country is basically a political economy. The political forces interact with the socio-economic forces to produce results and the outcome is dependent on the mix of such forces from time to time. Of late political forces have become quite strong and have sometimes played a dominant role much greater than that played by other forces and impact of such a role has not always proved to be beneficial as judged from the socio-economic consequences. However, political forces form an integral part of the working of an economy and study of such forces help in realistic analysis. The present paper shows the process of political intervention in poverty alleviation programmes as seen in West Bengal. Before getting down to the main emphasis of this study it is essential to make some remarks about the various poverty alleviation programmes which are being implemented now. Also at the outset it would not be out of place to mention that all these programmes whose direct beneficiaries are the poorest of the poor including the landless labourers, village artisans, small and marginal farmers etc. have been taken into account in this study in so far as they form the target group. Thus, the programmes which have been studied with reference to political intervention are IRDP (Integrated Rural Development Programme), SCP (Special Component Plan), TSP (Tribal Sub-Plan), JRY (Jawahar Rozgar Yojana), NREP (National Rural Employment Programme), and RLEGP (Rural Landless Employment Guarantee Programme).

The poverty alleviation programmes can be broadly divided into two categories, such as programmes which aim at creating some asset for the beneficiaries which are durable and productive in nature and which provide a source of a regular income for them e.g. IRDP, SCP,

TSP and programmes such as JRY which aim at generating wage employment opportunities in the rural areas in order to provide some income to the beneficiaries.

Structural Set-up

Now coming to the implementation aspect of these programmes there can be two categories with reference to the implementing agencies and these two categories are congruous with the above two divisions.

The asset endowment programmes involve three agencies at the implementation plane viz., (a) the nodal agency, District Rural Development Agency (DRDA) in case of IRDP and the SC&ST (Scheduled Caste and Scheduled Tribe) Development Corporation in case of TSP and SCP, which are conduits of subsidy financing; (b) the financing agency i.e. the commercial banks/cooperative banks which are the loan financing agencies; and (c) the Panchayat Raj Institutions (PRIs) which are responsible for selection of beneficiaries and also provide the link between the beneficiary and the nodal agency as well as the banks.

The wage employment generation programmes involve only the PRIs as the executing and the disbursing agencies.

Coming down to the PRIs as they exist in West Bengal, there are three tiers of these institutions viz., the *zilla parishad* at the district level, the *panchayat samiti* at the block level and the *gram panchayat* at the village level.

Functional Set-up

After the description of the structural set up of the implementational agencies, the functional set up needs to be touched upon briefly. In case of asset endowment programmes, the DRDA and the SC and ST Development Corporation get the financial as well as the physical targets for the district and the same is divided into targets for the district which is further sub-divided into targets for each of the *panchayat samitis* which in turn divide their targets amongst each of the *gram panchayats*. The *gram panchayat* has the responsibility of selecting the beneficiaries on the basis of a beneficiary list supposed to have been prepared after a house-to-house survey. Though in the original IRDP guidelines this job is entrusted to the *gram sabha*, in West Bengal the same is done by the *gram panchayat*. The *gram panchayat* thus identifies the beneficiaries, organises joint camps with bank authorities, recommends and forwards the cases to the concerned banks through the *panchayat samiti*. Recommendation of the sabhapati of *panchayat samiti* is also required. On sanction of the scheme, the *panchayat samiti* moves the concerned nodal agency for releasing the subsidy money and after the bank receives the subsidy, the entire amount i.e. loan plus subsidy is disbursed amongst the beneficiaries by the *pradhan* of the *gram panchayat*.

In case of wage employment generation programmes, only JRY has been discussed here as programmes such as NREP and RLEGP have been merged into JRY. The allotment of fund by the Central Government to the State Government is done on the basis of population. The State Government allocates this fund amongst the various *zilla parishads* following the same criterion. The entire fund that the *zilla parishad* gets is divided amongst the *panchayat samitis* and the *gram panchayats* on the basis of the guidelines of JRY i.e. some schemes are to be implemented exclusively by the *gram panchayat* while the others by the *panchayat samiti* or the *zilla parishad* itself and therefore a portion of the fund is retained by the *zilla parishad*. Now all these agencies undertake various schemes on the basis of their annual action plan with identified sectors and priorities.

The Scope for Political Intervention

The simplest connotation that 'political intervention' can have is intervention by politicians. Considering this there can be two forms of political intervention — one direct and the other indirect. By indirect it means intervention from outside, or intervention from those who do not figure statutorily within any of the implementing organs of the schemes mentioned above for instance, intervention of an MLA or an MP at the *zilla parishad, panchayat samiti* or *gram panchayat* level or for that matter the intervention of local leaders belonging to various political parties in decision making when they are not members of the local bodies. By direct intervention, it is meant that decision making is guided by the dictates of some functionary ignoring merit or eligibility. This is an intervention from within for instance, the intervention by a member of a local body or that of an legislature at State or Central level at the platform of DPCC (District Planning Coordination Committee) which has all the MPs and MLAs of the district as members in fixing up priorities or selecting schemes for different areas.

An attempt is made below to explain the process of political intervention, both direct and indirect in poverty alleviation programmes in order to explain the role which such intervention can play. Following are the stages in the entire gamut of poverty alleviation programmes where there exists scope for political intervention, be it direct or indirect:

IRDP/SCP/TSP

— allocation of financial and physical targets
— house-hold survey for identification and enlisting of beneficiaries
— selection of beneficiaries
— monitoring of schemes
— recovery of loans.

JRY

— selection of schemes
— selection of sites
— fixing of priorities of schemes
— selection of beneficiaries
— supervision of schemes.

IRDP and Political Intervention

In case of IRDP and other self-employment programmes the allocation of targets for *panchayat samities* are based on total allocation for the district and the past performance of the *panchayat samiti*. Regarding total allocation of targets for panchayat samities (i.e. sub-allocation of the total district target) a major factor is their past performance besides incidence of poverty in the area and there exists little scope for political manouvering. Political intervention is initiated at the level of house-hold survey for enlisting the potential beneficiaries group-wise. This stage is a very crucial one as it is at this stage that a "group" of people can be included or excluded from the survey. The survey is done through the staff and officers of block administration but the households to be covered is decided by the *panchayat* members of the area, at least in practice if not on paper. In some districts of West

Bengal, before 1989-90, the survey was done in some multiples of the total physical target e.g. if the target for a *panchayat samiti* is 600 then the number of families to be surveyed would be 600 × 3 or 600 × 4 i.e. 1800 or 2400. There may be 4000 poor families in the area who deserve to be enlisted but since the number of families to be surveyed is fixed by DRDA there exists ample scope for 'influencing' the survey.

The survey is done in order to ascertain the various groups (income-wise) within the poorer people and the beneficiaries are deemed to be selected group-wise. Unless the poorest group is exhausted there exists a bar in selecting beneficiaries from next higher income groups. Hence, this 'influence' used in distorting the survey is very crucial. The *panchayat* members may 'declare' that there exists no poor family in the village belonging to the poorest of the poor category and so the list should include families of the next higher income category. The possibility of existence of a number of deserving poorest of poor families in the village can be ignored because of their different political party affiliation and preference can be given to those with distinct party affiliation as of the *panchayat* member — generally the ruling party. Any amount of monitoring from a distance would not ensure proper selection of beneficiaries according to guidelines. And, on paper, such selection may be proper and perfect.

The only solution to this kind of intervention exists in a total survey of each and every household of the village to eliminate any kind of 'selective' survey. A DRDA may go in for a total survey. However, even this may not be fullproof. After this was done, there remains considerable scope for discrepancies in the survey. The government officials doing the survey can have their own biases. They can be influenced by the local leaders. The economic status of a group of people can be intentionally lowered to bring them within the target group so as to make them eligible for the benefits. However, there has been some progress towards better selection process by surveys conducted on the basis of all households because even if economic status of some persons have been manipulated there are other poor households who have at last found a place in the list of potential beneficiaries after being ignored for years together.

The above is an example of a combination of both direct and indirect intervention. If by direct intervention from outside, the selection of beneficiaries could not be 'influenced', then by indirect intervention in the capacity of a *panchayat* member or *pradhan* or *sabhapati* 'influence' may be exerted in rejecting or selecting a beneficiary. The administrative response to this intervention can be general helplessness mainly because of the loopholes in the selection process. The BDO or the SDO can make efforts to ensure that an undeserving household or a person is not selected but they may find it difficult to eliminate the possibility of selection of a less deserving beneficiary at the cost of a more deserving beneficiary as the certification of *panchayat* is a must and the list of beneficiaries has to be 'approved' by the *gram panchayat*.

Monitoring of schemes can be done by the officials concerned without any political intervention though the excuse of political pressures may be used as a cover for poor monitoring. So far as recovery of loan is concerned again the role of political influence comes. Since the selection has been done on the basis of some "affiliation" criterion, there may or may not be a 'forceful' recovery through the same people. Thus in practice, the *panchayat* gives the loan and the government machinery has to recover them. However, the selection which has been influenced can act both ways i.e. the panchayat can be told that since they have selected the beneficiaries, they should assure proper recovery or alternatively, since they have selected the beneficiaries on some extraneous considerations it is difficult to expect them to exert real pressure on their own people. It all depends on the local administration as to how the situation can be perceived and exploited. In some areas both the administration and *panchayats* have worked as a team and excellent results have been achieved. Since resources are limited they have to be distributed on a selective basis. Though there exists considerable deficiencies in the process of selection leaving ample scope for political intervention, things can be managed with some tact and sincerity as the administration can easily ensure that the identification and selection of beneficiaries satisfies the criteria is not imperfect according to standards. The administration may not be in a position to ensure that all the deserving people receive the benefits of these schemes simultaneously but can easily ensure that no undeserving person is selected as a beneficiary.

JRY and Political Intervention

In case of JRY the probable areas of intervention have been spelt out earlier. Selection of schemes has to be done as per the guidelines of the

JRY i.e. fixed proportions of total allocation have been earmarked for various schemes e.g. 25 per cent for social forestry, 15 per cent for SC/ST beneficiaries, 35 per cent for economically productive assets etc. Thus, in selection of schemes the scope for political intervention is quite limited. Then there are constraints of topography and geography also. Here the administrators have a greater say because of the technical factors involved and the level of technical skills available locally. The main political intervention comes into picture during selection of areas or sites for implementation of these schemes. Here the resolution of the *panchayat* body is most sacrosanct and the only point which the administration can ensure is adherence to the earmarked allocation and strict observance of guidelines, for instance, in the category of economically productive asset the *panchayat* can be asked to go for only such schemes which are economically productive for the community at large, say, a minor irrigation project of shallow tube-well (STW) but so far as the site or sites for these STW are concerned the BDO or his superior officers have little option. It is here that political considerations by way of direct and indirect intervention assumes significance. Similarly while it is possible to ensure that a particular scheme under JRY if meant for SC/ST goes to the same group but the selection of the area is a crucial point where decisions are mostly taken by indirect political intervention. However, it is not fair to say that the administration is the only one institution to take decisions which are fair and unbiased and the political leaders, being elected representatives are mostly biased. The aim of the description given above is to identify the areas where considerations other than merit infiltrate in the process of decision-making.

It has already been explained that when the allocation of funds is limited and much less than that demanded the need arises of some kind of a selection process and in a well established *panchayati raj* like that of West Bengal, the responsibility of such selection essentially lies with the elected representatives.

Political Intervention and Role of Administrators

Now the question arises whether such political intervention always plays a negative and damaging role ? The answer is generally 'no' but in some cases 'yes'. In West Bengal, since it is more of indirect intervention than direct, because of the well-established *panchayati raj*, the political intervention appears to be less harmful. Moreover, it is inevitable too as the basic responsibility of implementation of the poverty alleviation schemes lies on the PRIs and the role of administration is to see as to how these schemes are being implemented and not where these schemes are being implemented.

The role of administration is to see that the benefits always go to a certain category of people and not to ensure who amongst the category should be receiving it. The administration should see that no undeserving person gets the benefit at the cost of a deserving person but when it comes to selection of a limited number of people from a group of deserving potential beneficiaries, it is not for the administration to settle as to who amongst the deserving potential beneficiaries should be selected. Since the responsibility lies on the elected representatives of people in the *panchayats* and it is they who are ultimately answerable to people; there is no reason to believe that their selection will always be biased. The administrative responses to this kind of statutory political intervention is always positive but the problem starts surfacing only when the intervention is beyond 'statutory' limits or is 'extra-statutory'.

The village *panchayats* have to be endowed with such powers and authority as may be necessary to enable them to function as units of self-government. The public participation at the block and village level is mainly through elected representatives of the public. A democratic structure of administration from district downwards is necessary for meaningful popular participation. The Balwant Rai Mehta study team had also recommended constitution of statutory elective local bodies with the necessary resources, power and authority devolved on them and a decentralised administrative system working under their control. It has been noticed with ample evidence that wherever the *panchayati raj* bodies have been actively involved, the implementation of rural development programmes has been better and the selection of beneficiaries and designing of schemes have been more satisfactory. Therefore, it is generally accepted that various programmes of rural development will become realistic and meaningful only if people's representatives are actively involved in the local level planning, design formulation and implementation of these schemes and in selection of beneficiaries in the anti-poverty and employment programmes. The World Conference on Agrarian Reforms and Rural Development held in 1979 has also recommended the delegation of increasing responsibility for decision-making in rural development activities to institutions of local government. Various experts and study teams have advocated for a *gram sabha* for every village consisting of all the voters of the village and which would be responsible for identification of beneficiaries under poverty alleviation programmes like IRDP, RLEGP etc. However as has been mentioned elsewhere in this note, the concept of *gram sabha* has been replaced by *gram panchayat* in West Bengal and this has resulted in a distinct indirect political intervention in the selection process. Thus, while nobody in administration can undermine the role played by the local political leaders in the entire gamut of rural development including poverty alleviation programmes one has to accept that aberrations are bound to occur whenever the resources are less than the requirement.

Some Reflections on Political Intervention

Therefore, while indirect political intervention is bound to be there in a State like West Bengal in every sphere of rural development the reactions of the administrators will vary as per the political ethos and culture of the area. When the intervention is blatant, the administrative response to counter that intervention ought to be there. So far as direct political intervention is concerned nothing substantial can be bargained through it in such a strong *panchayat* system but it keeps a check on the whimsical and authoritarian trends cropping up within the PRIs. Therefore, at times limited direct intervention is also welcomed by the administration.

The development strategy is aimed at a direct attack on the problems of poverty, unemployment and regional imbalances. The success of this depends on effective development administration on the one hand and on the other the involvement and participation of the people in the formulation and implementation process through elected grass-root level institutions, voluntary agencies as well as organisations of the poor. These help in enhancing the effectiveness of the poverty alleviation programmes, in minimising leakages and integration of these programmes with area development consistent with local needs.

It can be concluded that the political intervention is minimal in West Bengal so far as direct political intervention is concerned but it is quite substantial as far as indirect political intervention is concerned and this kind of a situation is typical to an area where democratisation process of decision-making has reached the grass-root level. The administrators therefore, do not take it as a hindrance to development administration and bear with it so far it does not develop into a authoritarian and monopolistic intervention and for this very reason checks and balances in the form of direct political intervention is needed at an equal pace, though the limits vary and so vary the administrative responses too.

PART FOUR

SOME VILLAGE PROFILES

7

VILLAGE PROFILES OF WEST CHAMPARAN: Some Field Realities

GOPAL IYER et al.

(The village profiles of West Champaran are based on the village reports of the Indian Civil Service officers who underwent training at the Foundation course, autumn, 1990 at the L.B.S. National Academy, Mussoorie. Amongst villages visited were Sathe, Harnatan, Lachnauta and Dhumariya.)

District Background

The West Champaran district has a population of 19.73 lakh (as per 1981 Census) of which 93 per cent is located in the rural areas. The scheduled castes (SC) constitute 14.79 per cent and the scheduled tribes (ST) 1.36 per cent of the total population. The density of population is 402 km^2 which indicates high density. The agricultural labourers constitute 48.78 per cent and cultivators 36.35 per cent of the total workers indicating predominantly agricultural base of the district. Of the total 127.61 million acres in the district, 57.63 per cent is net cultivable area, 6.19 per cent area is under forest. The district is well served by irrigation systems of Tirhut main canal, Don canal branch, Triveni canal, and Ghoda Singhan branch canal. Besides this, the underground water-table is very high which has enabled the induction of large number of electrically and diesel operated tubewells to augment irrigation. The level of mechanisation of agriculture places it among the developed districts of Bihar with 1298 tractors, 131 State inducted tubewells, 5326 private tubewells, 4011 diesel-operated and 118 electrically-operated pump-sets. The principal crop during kharif is paddy and during rabi is wheat. During 1989-90 the area under paddy was 1,80,125 hectares and under wheat was 1,15,025 hectares. The subsidiary crops during kharif were maize (5941 hectares), pulses (6420 hectares) and under rabi were maize (10325 hectares) potato (10524 hectares) and pulses (53463 hectares). Apart from paddy and wheat, sugarcane is the predominant commercial crop covering 59020 hectares area during 1989-90. The yield of paddy is favourable with 29.20 quintal/hectare but the yield of wheat is rather low with 17.96 quintal/hectare.

The yield of sugarcane is also low which works out to 55 quintals/hectare. The application of NPK is 66.2 kg/hectare during kharif and 90.6 kg/hectare during rabi seasons. The district has two subdivisions and 16 blocks. The western part of the district borders Nepal and Uttar Pradesh. Three such blocks are populated by a community known as *tharus* who have all the characteristics of a tribe but are not recognised as such. As large as 13 *panchayats* in Bagaha II, 6 *panchayats* in Ramnagar and 17 *panchayats* in Gaunaha have concentration of *tharu* population. The total population of *tharus* in the district is 1.33 lakhs.

Until independence, the district was a part of *zamindari* of the *Betiah raj*. Though the *zamindari* system was abolished after independence, landlordism continues unabated in the district which is the major bottleneck to progress. The abolition of *zamindari* system did not make any difference in pattern of land concentration in the district. Even the Land Ceiling Act of 1961 could not make any dent into it. However, the peasant movement in this district during the 60s and 70s exerted some pressure on the administration as a result of which part of the lands of the big landlords were taken away under the land ceiling legislation of 1972. Apart from the administrative laxity and delays, the liberty enjoyed by the landlords to take recourse to courts has reduced the effectiveness of the land ceiling legislation. The weak implementation of land ceiling legislation in this district is apparent from the fact that according to official statistics 34063.31 acres is lying under dispute in various courts.

VILLAGE SATHE*

1

Pattern of land holding in village Sathe was highly skewed and 5000

1. * Rajesh Das, Sanjukta Pattnaik and Trisaljit Kochar

acres of land was owned by a single person who lived in Betiah. In the village there was a clear distinction of residential areas segregated on the basis of caste. The outskirts were dominated by the high caste people who were also economically better off. As far as the structure of houses was concerned, the high caste houses were made of bricks (even marble was used in some cases). They had a courtyard and each household had an individual handpump. In the families of the higher castes, children were by and large immunised and hygiene was good, sanitation quite proper and people were health conscious and spent a considerable amount on doctors and medicines.

However, this was not the case with the lower caste poor people. Children looked malnourished and none of them were immunised though the parents knew about the immunisation programme but they could not afford it. Similarly none of the children went to school from *harijan basti* except a few families who owned certain amount of land. In the Harijan caste, there was almost complete illiteracy and even children were working as agricultural labourers. Some of them who went to Punjab and Haryana during lean seasons were economically better off than others. Ration cards had been provided to them but never had they been provided with any ration. The public distribution system was at its lowest ebb.

Only one hand-pump existed in the village which was out of order. A number of complaints had been lodged which had fallen on deaf ears and all attempts to get it repaired were in vain. The water had to be brought from a local school which was at a distance.

Very few children of poor families went to school, mostly because they could not afford it and they also used children as a source of earning. They got Rs.10 to Rs.12 per day or 3 kg of paddy *(dhan)* for working for 8 hours in the fields each day. The paddy was sold for Rs.1.50 to Rs.2 per kg. For half of the month they were unemployed and lived off the money they procured by selling the paddy. There were elements of untouchability among the villagers. In lower castes, even women went out to work. They had an almost equal status with men and earned equal amount. But higher up in the caste hierarchy, women become confined to houses and were not allowed to go out of the house for education or job purposes.

Child marriage was very much prevalent. Girls at an age of around 5 years and boys at an age of around 10 years got married but the *gauna* ceremony (departure of the bride to in law's house) occurred much later. Size of dowry was exorbitant.

The various constraints faced by the children and their families led to very low enrolment in schools. Some of these were poverty leading to child labour, illiteracy of parents, lack of study culture, education not seen as a felt need and a feeling of 'apathy' which led to a feeling that it was beyond their scope.

The condition of primary school was incredible. More than 50 per cent of the teachers were not interested and negligent towards their duty resulting in further apathy on the part of students and deteriorating standards of primary education. It was learnt that for the past 12 years, the primary school had not been visited even once by the concerned school inspectors. Provisions provided by the government for economically and socially backward children did not reach them on time. The text-books and other materials reached the school quite late.

Regarding the high school in Sathe, the building of the school was in a dilapidated condition and was badly in need of repair. The black-boards needed polishing as nothing could be written on them. A hostel building was built 2 years back which was already falling apart. Scholarship was provided only to SC and ST students and there was no such provision for poor and meritorious children belonging to other castes. Another important observation made in this regard was the way in which the residential schools in the rural areas — *navodaya vidhyalayas* were manipulated by the urban elites with rural base. This resulted in rural children being deprived of this facility.

There was no primary health centre or any government dispensary but there were two private doctors. As far as health and immunisation was concerned the villagers said that Rs.10 was charged from them for vaccination and they could hardly afford this luxury especially when they had to go hungry for days together.

As far as Jawahar Rojgar Yojana (JRY) is concerned it was reported that till date no work had been done and even the money had not reached the *mukhia* from the district headquarters. In this village under the SC and ST rehabilitation programme of Indira Awas Yojana, some *pucca* houses had been built only 2 years back and they had already collapsed. The villagers observed that visits by the government officials were rare. Even if they arrived they wined and dined with the *mukhia* or *sarpanch* and had no communication with the ordinary people. No voluntary organisation was working in this village.

There were three other villages bordering Sathe village. Gulabnagar, Simri and Dharampura. These were comparatively poorer villages. There too agricultural labour was the most common occupation. Illiteracy and poverty were rampant and standards of health, hygiene and sanitation were of very low quality.

VILLAGE DHUMARIYA*

2

Village Dhumariya is also known as Dhumariya estate or the Dhumariya *darbar*, the appellation being a carry over from the British times. The village is located near the foothills of the Himalayas and has a population of around 2000 people.The village lies 3 kilometres off of the main road and the connection is by means of a *kutcha* road which is in a deplorable condition. The female/male ratio of the village is of the order of 950 : 1000. The bulk of the population is made up of the so-called 'backward classes' like *kurmi, telis* and *mallah*. They constitute 70 per cent of the population. The Harijans form about 25 per cent, while the upper castes constitute around 5 per cent of village population. The village is geographically separated into three blocks called *tolas*. The bulk of the population lives in the main block. The central place of this block is the *zamindar*'s manor like house. The Harijans live in a separate *tola*. The inhabitants of the village are Hindus by religion. There is almost no caste discrimination against scheduled castes and there is free intermixing of castes. The only aspect of discrimination is that a scheduled caste is not allowed to visit the inner room of the temple. He can only pray from the outer room.

The village still has a highly inequitable distribution of land and this is reflected in the pattern of land holdings. The *zamindar* owns about 800 acres of a total of 1050 acres of land in the village. There are about five families who have a landholding of about 12 to 15 acres. About 50 families mainly *Harijans* are landless. The pattern of land holding provides an indication of the power structure in the village which is highly lop-sided in character, socio-economic power being concentrated in the hands of the *zamindar*. Except for a negligible portion, the entire land is under cultivation. The cultivated area is irrigated by means of a canal. There are channels made in the fields for irrigation purposes and no tube-wells exist. Only the *zamindar* has tractors. There are two small sized ponds which are for the exclusive use of the *zamindar*. The others employ traditional methods of farming. The main crops grown are sugar-cane, paddy and wheat. The land is fertile and the yield of all the crops is much above the national average.

---

2. * Anirudh Tewari, Manoj Ahuja, Mukhmeet Singh and Charanjit Singh

The villagers, in general, are extremely poor and live on subsistence level. The small and marginal farmers are slightly better off than the landless labourers. Since there is no alternate form of employment, the villagers are required to work on the fields of the *zamindar*. Some of the villagers have cows, buffaloes and goats and they sell their milk in the nearby town. Some of the peasants have gone to Punjab and have been able to improve their economic conditions than the many others living in the village. Quite a number of labourers expressed their wish to go to Punjab to improve their economic conditions, in spite of the disturbed conditions existing there.

It is encouraging to find that there is no communal tension in the villages. The Muslims who are 5 per cent of the village population live with the Hindus in perfect communal harmony and even celebrate festivals together.

The family is male dominated but women *vis-a-vis* men are not so badly placed. Some of them work in the fields, apart from attending their household work. Dowry is prevalent and is a function of the status of the boy's family. Child marriage at a very early age is quite common. Most of the people interviewed, favoured the birth of a boy to a girl in their family. The literacy amongst them is low. The village women make beautiful baskets made of *munja* grass which grows wild all over the place. If proper marketing facilities can be provided for the sale of this, it will provide some additional income to the villagers. The input cost of the material used is nominal and selling the basket for a lucrative price in the cities should not be a problem.

A middle school is situated in the main village. There are 14 teachers on the staff and there are 200 students enrolled. The school has 8 rooms. The teachers are found to be quite regularly absenting themselves from duty. The building and furniture are in a dilapidated condition. The school drop out rate for girls is higher than that of boys.

The primary health centre (PHC) is in a deplorable condition. The stock of medicines is inadequate and poor. Though it has provisions for immunisation they generally remain out of supply. The doctor who is supposed to visit the PHC fortnightly is quite irregular. The PHC is manned by a compounder who is just a graduate and untrained in the field of medical science.

The villagers are forced to take loans in case of marriages, illness in the family etc. Loan is provided by the zamindar and other money-lenders with smaller holdings. The general rate of interest vary from 25 per cent to 60 per cent per annum. However, the problem of indebtedness is not quite acute and generally over a period of time a debtor is able to pay back his debt. A *gramin bank* which serves this village along with 7 other adjoining ones is also located in the village. It attempts at mobilising small savings and disburses loans for government programmes like IRDP (Integrated Rural Development Programme) and monitors the beneficiaries for repayment of loans.

The village is fully electrified. It also has a supply of clear drinking water from two wells constructed under the JRY programme and some 12 hand-pumps of which only half work.

The Minimum Wages Act is blatantly violated. The villagers for an 8 hour of work per day are given 2.7 to 3.7 kg of paddy which is less than the legal minimum wages of Rs.16.50 applicable at present. Even in the government schemes such as JRY the villagers are paid Rs. 15 instead of the stipulated wage per day. The villagers are aware of the Minimum Wages Act, but are helpless. The men and women, however, get equal wages.

In the real sense of the term, no peasant can be classified as a bonded labour as he is free to leave the land and seek work whenever he wants. But because of availability of surplus labourers and absence of alternative employment opportunities, the poor have to work only for the *zamindar*, who pays them wages which are much below the legal minimum wage. Some of the landless labourers work as sharecroppers. The *zamindar* leases out a piece of land generally less then one acre. The peasant cultivates the land and gives the zamindar his fixed share which is 44 *maunds* per *bigha*.

Another prominent village institution is the *gram panchayat*, which is headed by a *mukhia* who happens to be the *zamindar* of the village and also an MLA from a nearby constituency. The members of *panchayat* are supposed to be elected periodically, the last election being held in 1978. Besides implementing government programmes like Jawahar Rojgar Yojana, the *panchayat* also exercises certain judicial powers but its decisions can only be implemented if both the disputing partners agree to it.

The administration for the village is a far off entity. The villagers believed that the officials are hand in league with the *zamindar*. They also stated that not much official help is forthcoming in getting loans for IRDP, fighting court cases or in other matters.

, JRY has been ensured as a scheme to provide jobs to landless labourers during the lean period with hundred per cent government assistance. Following are the schemes which have been take up by the government for Dhumariya village from 1988 onwards:

(i) brick roads;
(ii) planting of *Sisham* tree;
(iii) construction of *pucca* wells;
(iv) construction of *sulabh shauchalyas* (cheap toilets); and (v) repairing of irrigation channel.

Most of the schemes have been implemented in a very poor manner. Under JRY, a road was laid connecting village with the main road. Just after a year of its laying the road is in a very bad condition with pot holes. Of two wells constructed in the village only one is functional. The only promising aspect may be found in *Shisam* tree plantations which are now 2 years old and are in good shape due to their proper care by panchayat.

VILLAGE HARNATAN*

3

The village Harnatan is situated at the heart of the Harnatan panchayat. It is connected in the north by Mahadeva village, in the south by canal, in the east by Beriakhurd village and in the West by Harnatad bazaar. The village is almost in the foothills of the Nepal border. The thick forests start from about 2.5 km from the village. The topography of the village is plain with black clay loam soil. The village has about 175 acres of land. The soil is fertile with high water-holding capacity. The climate of the area is sub-tropical with cold winter and hot and sultry summer. The village is entirely inhabited by *Tharoo* tribal community. The Tharoos who have similar ethno-cultural identities and living styles as those of other tribals have however not been included in the category scheduled tribe. There are 51 Tharoo families staying in the village. Most of the families are small and marginal farmers and landless labourers. The size of land-holding and number of families owning them are given below:

Size of land holding	No. of families
No land	12
Less than 1 acre	15
1-5 acres	10
5-10 acres	9
more than 10 acres	5

3. * Alkesh Sharma, Tejender Singh and Anil K. Gupta

Almost the entire land is rainfed except for big landlords who have shallow wells for irrigating rabi wheat. About 30 years back every household in the village had land for cultivation. Most of them have now been alienated by the *bajis* (outsiders) who have taken hold of the lands. Poor landless labourers get employment only during the planting and harvesting season. Now due to expansion of area under sugarcane these opportunities are also going down. They get employment for 60 to 75 days in a year. Rest of the time, they either migrate or collect forest produce.

Access to forest produce has reduced over the years. The forest officials are supposed to have a nexus with contractors who take away a major chunk of minor forest produce. These poor villagers who earlier used to collect fuel-wood, *sabai* grass, *moonj* grass and leaves (for plates) are now unable to get those due to strict forest laws.

Paddy is the main kharif crop grown in the area. It is cultivated from June to October-November. Some of the farmers grow wheat in rabi season while most other leave their fields fallow. Big farmers have started growing sugarcane in their fields and they take as many as five ration crops. They also grow some pulses. Earlier *khesari dal* was also cultivated but now other pulses are grown like arhar and lentil. Poor farmers also grow minor millets like *kondo* on their fields. Kitchen gardening is a common feature in the village.

Most of the farmers follow old methods and implements for crop cultivation and tillage. Bullock-ploughs are the most common features except for one farmer in the village who has a tractor. The poor farmers use traditional varieties of seeds. However, the progressive and better off farmers have started growing HYV seeds using chemical fertilizers in their fields.

Tharoos are basically farmers. They remain attached to the land in the village. The occupations range from farming, agricultural labourer, mason work, making of cups/plates from leaves, rope making and others. Apart from this the village has two teachers, one peon and three who have joined the army. One villager is also a graduate in that village. Tharoo community in the village has traditionally been rearing animals. They have bullocks, buffaloes, cows, goats and poultry birds. The affluence of a family in addition to his landholding is also determined by the size of his cattle wealth. Big landlords in the village have many pairs of bullocks and cattle which form important sources of milk, draught power, tillage operations and farm yard manure/ compost manure and fuel.

Since there is only one community in the village, there exists caste harmony. There is no well defined caste structure within the Tharoo community but there is class differentiation. Big Tharoo landlords sit exclusively with other landlords during social ceremonies and functions. However the whole community works for each other irrespective of class differences. Child marriage is a common phenomenon in the village. Every girl child gets married before she attains the age of 10 years. Same is true of a boy before attaining the age of 13 years. Of late, educated boys prefer late marriage. Widow remarriage is common. It is difficult to find a single unmarried girl above the age of 10 years. The marriage of boys in early age is due to the fact that it becomes difficult to find suitable match later.

The villagers are non-vegetarian by habit. They serve non-vegetarian meals during religious and social functions. They worship all Hindu gods and they also have two special gods, namely *brahmasthanan* in the middle of the village and *dahar chandi* at the entrance of each Tharoo village. They celebrate most of the Hindu festivals and in addition have their own festivals like *fagua, budhwa atwar* and others. Their living styles are simple. They have a peculiar culture *khasi khai* in which the females go in procession with the bride to the bridegroom's village.

There is a *gumasta* in the village who is a traditional apolitical leader of the village. He takes decisions with his *panchayat* on all socio-religious matters in the village. He is the person who should first be contacted if an outsider wishes to interact with the villagers and it is he who receives them after which the other villagers can interact.

The literacy percentage in the village is as low as 10.0 per cent. The female literacy is around 3.0 per cent Now villagers have realised the importance of literacy and are sending their children (both boys and girls) to school. None of the married old females in village are literate. There is a primary school in the village which has just one teacher and the number of boys and girls enrolled are almost equal in the villages. However, the standard of education is of a low quality and facilities are negligible. In addition to this, there is an evening school run by a local inhabitant to teach small children. The children come from their home at 6.00 p.m. every day and study till 8.00 p.m. They bring their own lanterns and mats to sit on the ground in front of the teacher's house. Due to better efforts of the teacher these children are more intelligent than those of the primary school. Some primary school children also study in this evening school.

Harnatan village doe not have a primary health centre. The medical facilities are negligible. The nearest health centre is about 1.5 km away at Harnatad bazar. There is no vaccination facility and about 90 per cent of children and pregnant mothers are not vaccinated. The health worker who visits that village quite infrequently charge Rs.5 per vaccination which is too high a rate for the poor villagers.

No family in the village has a ration card. They just receive sugar from PDS (public distribution system) shop which is managed by a *bania* in Harnatad bazar about one km from the main village. They are not aware of the other commodities which are also distributed through PDS. Since 9 months they have not received any sugar from the *bania*.

The village has a general problem related to the distribution of *pattas*. None of the poor landless families have got homestead *pattas* so far. Even the land which has been distributed to them under Land Ceiling Act is not in their possession. The officials demanded some money for issuing such *pattas*, which the poor villagers have not been able to pay.

Two bonded labourers could be identified in the village. They are working with the landlords in the same village within their community. The bonded labourers are attached to family of landlord for last many years. Their living conditions are really pathetic. Some characteristics of bondage which could be observed were element of force, loss of freedom of movement, getting less than the minimum wage and long hours of work.

As regards the performance of IRDP in the village it was found that only a few genuinely poor families were given IRDP loans. Most of the families identified and assisted were above the poverty line and hence, in the process many poor households were left out. The poor households who were not included in the programme mentioned that no proper household survey was conducted for selection of beneficiaries, the loans were got by *mukhia*'s group and they had no money to offer as bribes to the various functionaries of the system. Some of the beneficiaries were forced to sell their assets because of factors like asset of low quality, loss due to payment of bribes and funds required for social ceremonies and others. As regards JRY there were complaints of low wage payment at many places. The 60: 40 ratio of wage and material component was also not adhered to.

VILLAGE LACHNAUTA*[4]

Lachnauta is a fairly advanced village in the district. It is situated about 40 km away from the district headquarters at Betiah. According to the 1981 Census the population of the village was 1491 which has now increased to 2000. The village has an approach road (constructed under JRY). It has a railway station as well which is called Rameshwarnagar. Trains plying between Betiah (district headquarters) and Raxaul (on Nepal border) stop here.

In the village, people are highly caste-conscious. People from upper and lower castes do not freely interact with each other and there are feelings of antipathy among them towards each other. There is caste-wise spatial segregation where people from different castes live together in small settlements called tolas.

Class is parallel to caste where upper caste people are generally rich farmers or landlords while the lower caste people are mostly landless labourers.

The village has about 10-15 per cent Muslim population, the rest being Hindus. The Muslims live together in a separate *tola*. They are mostly engaged in washing, tailoring and agriculture. The village has a 400 year old Shiva temple with a pond and a 150-year old mosque too. There is fairly amiable relation prevailing between the two communities in the village. Some enlightened youth from the poorer sections are working fervently for better relations between the two communities and taking care of any attempts to drive a wedge between them.

Sugarcane and rice are the two most important crops of the village and in fact, of the whole region. Besides other crops like wheat, oilseeds, pulses (mainly *arhar* and *chana*) vegetables are also grown. The village has a few orchards with trees of mango and *leechi*. Besides that, bamboo and *sheesham* trees are available in abundance.

Agriculture is the main occupation for most of the labour force of the village. People in possession of land till their own lands while the others work as agricultural labourer. However, few of them have begun to shift to other jobs which are more paying than agricultural labourer. Around four to five households are engaged in blacksmiths, a couple of families are involved in carpentry and two families are running diesel

4. * G.R. Meena, Deepak Agrawal and Kamal Dayani

owing to the large migration of people from Zanskar (Ladakh) to that region. In Lahaul and Kinnaur too Buddhism is prevalent, although Hinduism is growing stronger in these areas. The dominant religion in H.P. is Hinduism (95.8%) followed by Islam (1.6%), Buddhism (1.2%) and Sikhism (1.2%).

Most villages continue to follow the joint family system (about 70 per cent in Trilokpur, Sirmaur) but this system is decreasing in popularity in the less backward areas. In Jaddera, which is a comparatively backward village of Chamba, the bonds of the joint family have not weakened and this system is common. The economic rationality of the joint family system, in that it does not lead to excessive subdivision and fragmentation of holdings, is also realised.

One of the reasons for the decline of the joint family system is the near disappearance of the practice of polyandry in the villages of H.P. This practice used to prevail in the border regions of H.P. (Simla, Kinnaur, Lahaul and Spiti) and in the lower region of the Giri valley (Sirmaur). While polyandry may be morally indefensible and socially regressive, it can be defended on the economic grounds of preventing over-population and sub-division in areas with insufficient agricultural land. In the village Kuar (Simla distt.) polyandry in the form of one woman marrying several brothers, who form a group of 'fraternal husbands', is still common — but elsewhere it is a rare instance.

While women are subservient to men, especially in marriage, their status is better than in most other parts of the country. Widow remarriage is disapproved of only amongst Brahmins and the Rajputs (otherwise, especially amongst the scheduled castes, it is quite common). At the time of marriage dowry is usually not demanded, but some articles are given as befitting ones *haiseeyat*. Those who demand cash may face social boycott ! The *Jhagra* or the *Gaddar* is a typical *Pahari* marriage ceremony performed by the backward castes. It is initiated by the boy's side and is conducted informally, without the traditional *phere*. Married women have a special status in religious ceremonies. Very few women are covered under the IRDP and TRYSEM (Training of Rural Youth for Self Employment) but *mahila mandals* have been set up in villages to promote and give information and skills about health and hygiene, kitchen gardening, simple crafts, small savings, family planning, etc. By and large the women of H.P. are hard working, both in household activities as well as in the field. They are valued as tremendous assets, which accounts for their relatively better status as compared to many other parts of the country.

In some areas (in the higher regions of H.P.) the prospective groom may even have to compensate the bride's parents adequately — a sort of reverse dowry!

Education

Education is given a major focus in the villages of H.P. All villages under consideration have atleast one primary school, and eleven (out of 13) have high schools. (These are often constructed through JRY schemes.) In Jaddera, Chamba, there has been a continuous increase in enrolment from 1981 to 1987. The enrolment of female children is also encouragingly high. The drop-out rate is minimal in primary school, but in middle school the girls virtually discontinue their studies. Another problem is the poor quality of teaching. While the literacy rate in H.P. has shot up remarkably, adult education and vocational education need to be emphasised as well.

Conclusion

Let us summarise some of the broad patterns and characteristics of the villages studied:

1. The proportion of cultivated land is low; landholdings are usually small and their distribution is not very skewed. There are not as many landless labourers as in U.P., Bihar, etc.
2. The proportion of irrigated land is low; in the higher regions it is usually nil.
3. The cropping pattern is very similar in most areas (except for the remote hilly regions). Maize and wheat are the most common kharif and rabi crops respectively.
4. Agriculture is the dominant occupation.
5. Horticulture is another important activity. Fruit processing industries have tremendous scope. Marketing strategies are limited and the problem of middlemen is quite acute.
6. Animal husbandry is another area in which there is a lot of scope for improvement — especially in the quantity of milk production and the quality of sheep wool.
7. The new areas of economic activity such as sericulture, bee-keeping and social forestry offer good prospects for growth and employment.

TABLE 8.1: Tabulated Data on Villages

Index No.	Village	District	Population (1981 Census) Total			IRDP (%)	HHs (*1)	Land Holding Pattern (per centHH) (*2)						Crops (*3)		Other(*4)						
				Sex Ratio	Literacy per cent			Landless	0-1	1-2	2-4	4-10	ha	Kharif	Rabi (*5)	Irrig.	E	PO	B	D	PS	HS
A.1.	Dhara	Bilaspur	548	1008	—	15	(47)	3	32	23	27	15	[2.37]	M,U	W,G	Nil	Y	Y	N	Y	Y	Y
A.2.	Panthelra	Bilaspur	1842	—	—	—	—	8	75	12	5	0		M,R	W,G	Nil	Y	Y	Y	Y	Y	Y
A.3.	Majwar	Mandi	159	810	—	—	—	0	33	67	0	0		R,M	W	17	Y	Y	N	Y	Y	Y
A.4.	Lapas	Mandi	253	976	—	10	—	0	89	11	0	0	[0.61]	M,P	W,Ba	Nil	Y	N	Y	N	Y	Y
A.5.	Kot	Bilaspur	1913	857	—	14	—	8	80	12	0	0	[0.58]	M,R	W	26	Y	Y	Y	Y	Y	Y
A.6.	Bagsaid	Mandi	7900	1080	—	18	—	0	71	23	5	0.4	[0.88]	M,P	W,Ba	54	Y	Y	Y	Y	Y	Y
A.7.	Kallol	Bilaspur	745	970	—	—	—	—	—	—	—	—	—	Ml,Ga	W,G,Mu	Nil	Y	Y	Y	Y	Y	Y
A.8.	Jachh	Mandi	256	1150	30 (m-50,f-16)	67	—	0	72	23	5	0	[0.86]	R,P,Pe,M	W,Ba,Mu	100	Y	Y	N	Y	Y	Y
B.1.	Trilokpur	Sirmaur	1071	915	44 (m-53,f-34)	46	—	1	67	32	0	0	[0.82]	P,O,C	W,Mu,Ba	Nil	Y	Y	N	I	Y	Y
B.2.	Ghaniara	Kangra	2259	938	48 (m-60,f-35)	23	(32)	12	87	1	0	0	[0.45]	M,R	W,L	51	Y	Y	N	Y	Y	Y
B.3.	Jaddera	Chamba	642	—	15	15	(68)	31	50	12	7	0	[0.64]	M,K,Mo,Ra	W,Ba,Ms	16	I	Y	Y	N	Y	N
B.4.	Manwa	Bilaspur	680	1018	47	4	—	1	75	19	5	0	[0.81]	M	W,Mu,G	Nil	Y	Y	N	Y	Y	N
C.1.	Kuar	Simla	2300	—	16	negligible		—	—	—	—	—	—	M,K,Ch	Mh	Nil	N	N	N	Y	Y	Y

Note:

*1 Figures in brackets indicate percentage of households(HHs) below the poverty line.

*2 None of these villages has any holding above 10 hectares. Figures in [] brackets indicate the average size of a landholding. For this purpose the mid-points of landholding classes are considered.

*3 M=maize, W=wheat, U=urad, G=gram, R=rice, Ba=barley, P=potato, Ml=malla, Ga=gandam, Mu=mustard, Pe=peas, O=onion, C=chillies, L=linseed, K=kodra, Mo=moong, Ra=rajma, Ms=masar, Ch=chaullai, Mh=mushroom.

*4 E=electrification, PO=post-office, B=bank, D=dispensary, PS=primary school, HS=high school; Y=yes, N=no, I=incomplete.

*5 Irrigation as percentage of net sown area.

Source: See References.

REFERENCES

This village profile is based on 8 village reports and 4 socio-economic surveys prepared during village attachments by Indian Civil Service officers under training at the L.B.S. National Academy of Administration. They are as follows.

Village Reports, 1986:	Dhara (Bilaspur)
	Panthelra (Bilaspur)
	Majwar (Mandi)
	Lapas (Mandi)
	Kot (Bilaspur)
	Bagsaid (12 villages)(Mandi)
	Kallol (Bilaspur)
	Jachh (Mandi)
	Kuar (Simla)
Socio-Economic Surveys:	Trilokpur (Sirmaur), 1987
	Ghaniara (Kangra), 1989
	Jaddera (Chamba), 1987
	Manwa (Bilaspur), 1987

Economic Review of *Himachal Pradesh*, 1989.

9

RURAL SCENARIO OF MANIPUR

RAHUL RASGOTRA

The present study sketches a rural scenario of Manipur on the basis of socio-economic surveys of four villages of Manipur, viz. Nungsai Chiru, Thanlon, Komlathabi-Heigrutampak and Lambui. These surveys were carried out in 1987 and all the four surveys relate to tribal villages.[1] About 27 per cent of the population of Manipur consists of scheduled tribes, who are mainly concentrated in the five hill districts. There is a discernible difference between the levels of development of the hill districts and the three districts located in the valley. The profile will concentrate on four aspects-breakdown of the traditional economy, demography, unemployment and poverty alleviation programmes.

Changes in the Traditional Economy

The basic characteristics of a tribal economy are those of a subsistence and a self-sufficient economy; communal ownership of land; and economic exchanges characterised by reciprocity. There are a number of factors which operate to alter these traditional characteristics such as the development of transport facilities, introduction of modern technology, migration of outsiders into the tribal area, population growth, State activity and education. We shall focus on the development of transportation as the single most important factor.

Prof. C. Von Furer-Haimendorf has shown in the course of his comparative studies of the tribal societies of Andhra Pradesh and Arunachal Pradesh[2] that the nature of change in the tribal economy could be for better or for worse with the development of transport depending on whether the following conditions obtain such as (i) a high level of education; and (ii) restrictions on the entry of non-tribals into the tribal area.

Both these conditions are adequately satisfied in the case of these villages and in the State of Manipur as a whole. In spite of this the per capita income of Manipur is only two-thirds of the national average according to the Seventh Five Year Plan for Manipur.[3] The following observations will try to address this issue, *inter alia*:

Table 9.1 below shows the quality of road, the technological level of the village economy and the presence or absence of the phenomenon of migration from/into the village. The hypothesis is that given the high level of education and the restrictions on the entry of outsiders into the state, the construction of roads should lead to the transition to more 15 productive agricultural economy through exposure to more advanced methods and thereby to an enhancement of standard of living of the people without fear of exploitation by outsiders moving into the area.

TABLE 9.1: Roads, Technology and Migration in the Four Village

	Nungsai-Chiru	Thanlon	Komlathabi & Heigrutampak	Lambui
Roads	No road to distt. or block hqs	Poor quality road to distt. hqs	Located just to off the state highway	On main road between Imphal & Ukhrul
Technology	rudimentary dependent on *jhum*	dependent on *jhum*; 9 families in wetland agriculture	26/135 families depend only on jhum	most families in wetland agriculture
Migration	no outsiders limited emigration	19/25 village shops owned by outsiders	no outsiders	most indebted to local moneylenders

Note: distt. and hqs stand for district and headquarter respectively.

It will be seen from the above table that as one moves from Nungsai-Chiru to Lambui the quality of the road connection between the village and the district or block headquarters progressively improves. Keeping this in mind the following observations may be made:

(i) The degree of dependence on *jhum* cultivation decreases. All families in village Nungsai-Chiru practice *jhum*, whereas most families in Lambui practice settled, wetland-type agriculture. The few who stuck to *jhum* did so for the reason that it has a certain religious association. In the intermediate region,

Thanlon has only 9 families in wetland agriculture whereas Komlathabi-Heigrutampak has only 26 families entirely dependent on *jhum*. This shows clearly that the construction of a road leads to an improvement in technology.

(ii) Notwithstanding the regulatory framework, the presence of migrants in the villages shows a significant increase with improvement in quality of road. Thus, Nungsai-Chiru with no road connection with either block or district headquarters has no outsiders in the village, while in Thanlon, of 25 shops 19 are owned by outsiders. Furthermore, in Lambui we find that most families are indebted to local moneylenders — a common enough phenomenon in tribal societies exposed to the outside world in other parts of India without the benefit of inner line regulations restricting the entry of non-tribals into tribal areas. However, note must be taken here of the exception in the form of Komlathabi-Heigrutampak where no outsiders are present.

(iii) Although it is not shown in Table 9.1, the farmers of all the villages under reference show a high degree of awareness of the existence of modern seed-water-fertilizer technology, a negligible number of them have actually gone in for it. Two factors may account for this. One, the irrigated area in the entire State is less than 20 per cent of the cultivated area.[4] Two, the distribution network for supplying seeds, etc., to the farmers does not exist nor does any training and extension network operate, atleast in the four villages considered in this study. In addition, the structure of landholding is such that a less productively settled agriculture (relative to the potential generated by the new technology) is also not capable of supporting the population dependent on it, which in turn creates an opportunity for outside moneylenders to move in.

In the villages dependent on jhum the land is owned by the village chief who assigns plots to individual farmers at the beginning of the season. Traditionally the chief received a tribute in kind, however, with the advent of settled cultivation this system is now breaking down. In Thanlon, for example, the chief was paid a tin of rice from the final output by every farmer, but this practice is observed now more in the breach.

Demography

The State has a compound rate of growth of population of about 2.9 per cent per annum which is considerably higher than the 2.2 per cent for the country as a whole during 1981-90. In the villages under consideration no data are available on population growth. However, data are available for household size, which is presented alongwith certain other relevant variables.

The normal hypothesis is that a high level of education stimulates, among other things, a reduction in the rate of population growth and correspondingly in the family size. We examine this hypothesis below (Table 9.2).

TABLE 9.2

	Nungsai-Chiru	Thanlon	Komlathabi & Heigrutampak	Lambui
Household Size	5.7	n.a.	4	3.8
Education	57% literacy 2 schools	4 schools	4 schools & 1 college	1 Jr. high school & Navodaya Vidyalaya
Health Facilities	none	PHC exists but poor service	PHC exists	PHC exists

Note : PHC stands for primary health centre; n.a. stands for data not available.

From the above table it appears that the level of literacy or the quality of educational facilities seems to bear no correlation with the size of the household. In Nungsai-Chiru, the literacy rate is 57 per cent and there exist 2 schools with adequate facilities and the household size is 5.7, while in Lambui, where there exists only one junior high school and an upcoming Navodaya Vidyalaya still operating out of temporary structures, the household size is 3.8. The explanation for this interesting fact seems to lie in the three points discussed below:

There is a decrease in household size as the degree of dependence on *jhum* decreases. This is intuitively plausible as *jhum* cultivation is a relatively more labour-intensive activity than settled, wetland agriculture and therefore families dependent on *jhum* are likely to value a larger family.

Again, the existence and quality of medical facilities could also serve to explain the observed pattern in the family size. For instance, no health facilities are available in Nungsai-Chiru at all while there exists a phc in Lambui. In the intermediate case of Thanlon, a PHC exists but very poor quality service is available in so far as no doctor is generally present.

We see quite clearly that family size decreases discernibly as we move across the row from Nungsai-Chiru to Lambui. In other words, family size decreases as accessibility of the village improves. This could conceivably be interpreted in a number of different ways — for example, improved accessibility means better agricultural technology which raises income and also leads to a smaller family size and a lower rate of population growth.

Unemployment

This is a major problem in the State. The number of persons on the live register of unemployment exchanges rose from 20,000 in 1974 to about 167,000 in 1983. There is virtually no large or medium industry in the State and therefore the genesis and the solution of the problem lies basically in improving the productivity of agriculture. We present and examine some of the basic features of the economy of the four villages under consideration in this profile below.

With regard to agriculture the following comments are in order:

(i) Except Komlathabi-Heigrutampak, all the other villages have atleast 70 per cent of the households engaged in agriculture. For the State as a whole about 67 per cent of the population is dependent on agriculture.

(ii) About the pattern of landholding it may be observed that the majority of holdings are between 1 and 3 acres in size, and the size of *jhum* plots is distinctly less than those of wetland agriculturists. This has clear implications for the ability of the economy to support a rapidly growing population in an environment in which industrial jobs are not forthcoming. It is imperative that these farmers adopt a more productive technology and it is equally imperative that the state stimulate such a transition by developing and extending distribution, training and extension networks.

(iii) Only one crop is taken in all cases every year which, given the small size of holdings, is patently inadequate. The cropping intensity needs to be increased.
(iv) The main crop everywhere is paddy. About 85 per cent of cultivated area in the State is under paddy.
(v) There is a uniform lack of irrigation facilities in these villages except in Komlathabi-Heigrutampak to some extent.

In respect of village industry the following observations can be made:

(i) The main village industries are weaving, blacksmiths and carpentry.
(ii) The technology used is in general traditional and suited to low volume production catering to home demands.
(iii) No marketing organisation has been established by the State for village handicrafts. Data from Thanlon shows that most the surplus produce is sold to the local traders, middlemen and/or private agents. The latter are often able to exploit the situation to their advantage as for example in Thanlon, the traders buy brooms made of plentiful forest grass by the tribals which is of little value to them and sell them essential commodities at high prices. This is facilitated by the fact that no public distribution system worth the name exists in the village.
(iv) The State has a good potential for development of agro-industries, especially rice mills, and weaving with improved technology.
(v) There exists a number of constraints to the development of village industry such as remoteness, lack of adequate finance, non-availability of sophisticated production and management technology and non-availability of electricity. Per capita consumption of electricity in Manipur is 12.4 kWh (1981-82) against an all India average of 135 kWh (1980-81).

A few emergent factors serve to further complicate the problem. First, with a greater awareness of the material culture of the outside world, the tastes of the younger generation in particular are changing. In Thanlon, we find that the youth prefer wearing jeans rather than traditional handmade garments. Seventy-five per cent of the households own wristwatches and about 40 per cent own transistors. This change in the pattern of demand will push the economy into a position of unequal exchange in so far as demand structure will favour products of the industrialised economy outside while the products offered for exchange will be undervalued. The second important problem is the fact that almost all those educated beyond the high school level seek jobs outside the village either in government or in industry.

Poverty Alleviation Programmes

The implementation of the poverty alleviation programmes (PAPs) is by and large indifferent. It suffers from the same sort of infirmities that beset these programmes in most other States. However some points of interest are discussed below:

> The selection of beneficiaries under the IRDP is done basically by the village chief or headman assisted by the village council where it exists. This procedure is no less prone to direct a significant part of the assistance to ineligible persons than other procedures used elsewhere. Among the other problems are high unit cost of assets and poor back-up support or maintenance of assets. For example, cattle provided under the programme frequently dies in the absence of veterinary care. It is also interesting to note that the bank component of total financial assistance package was not received at all in Thanlon. Further, no marketing facilities exist for disposal of production of newly established units.
>
> In Komlathabi-Heigrutampak out of 45 persons assisted in 1982-83, only four persons who were given fisheries continued to operate their schemes. All the rest of the schemes were defunct.
>
> There is unfortunately not much information on the response of the people to these schemes. Finally, the survey on Nungsai-Chiru brings out the importance of ethnic identity when the people ascribed the lack of government schemes in their village to the fact that the MLA from the area belonged to the Kuki tribe while the village was exclusively composed of the Chiru tribe.

Conclusion

The opening up of these areas by constructing roads leads to significant change in the society and in the economy of these villages. But we have seen that in order for the change to be beneficial the State must provide quickly a package of incentives/schemes for example irrigation facilities, marketing network, credit facilities, health facilities and cheap, adequate education, alongwith the construction of a road. This would perhaps also serve to contain the population growth problem as discussed earlier. Finally the unemployment problem calls for design and implementation of a suitable education system and also the expansion of irrigation and multicropping in agriculture.

REFERENCES

1. These surveys were carried out by Indian Administrative officers under training at the L.B.S. National Academy of Administration, Mussoorie.
2. C. Von Furer-Haimendorf, *The Tribes of India*, Oxford University Press, 1982.
3. *Seventh Five Year Plan 1985-90*, Government of Manipur.
4. *Ibid.*

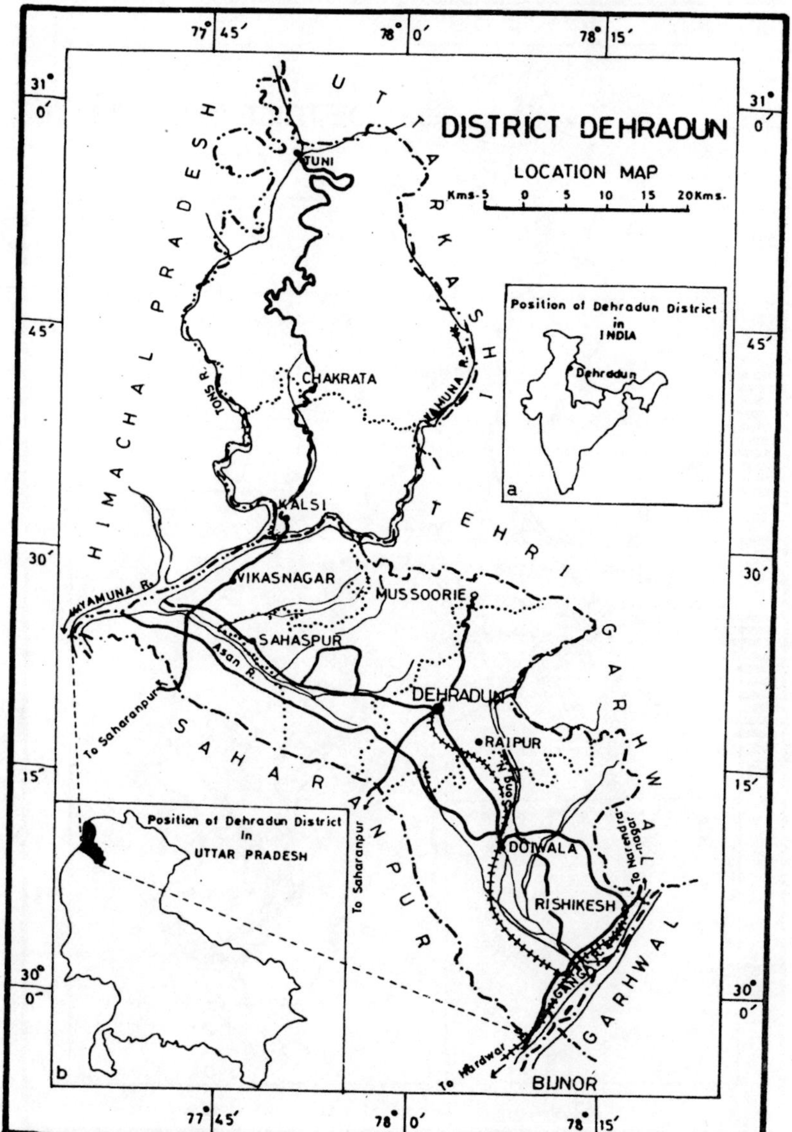
DISTRICT DEHRADUN
LOCATION MAP
Kms.5 0 5 10 15 20Kms.
Position of Dehradun District in INDIA
Dehradun
a
Position of Dehradun District In UTTAR PRADESH
b
UTTARKASHI
HIMACHAL PRADESH
TEHRI GARHWAL
SAHARANPUR
GARHWAL
BIJNOR
TUNI
CHAKRATA
KALSI
VIKASNAGAR
MUSSOORIE
SAHASPUR
DEHRADUN
RAIPUR
DOIWALA
RISHIKESH
TONS R.
YAMUNA R.
Asan R.
Song
GANGA R.
To Saharanpur
To Hardwar
To Narendra-nagar
77° 45′
78° 0′
78° 15′
31° 0′
45′
30′
15′
30° 0′

FIG. 10.1

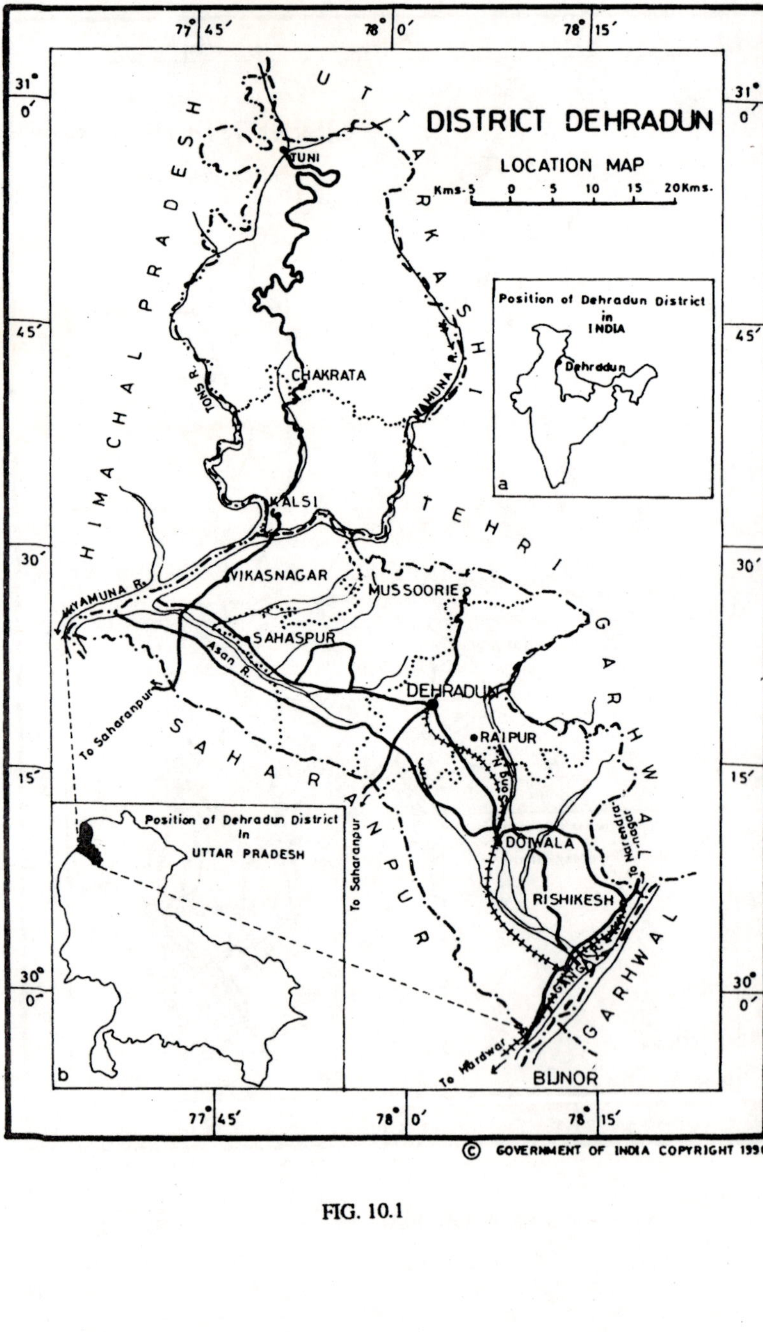
DISTRICT DEHRADUN
LOCATION MAP
Kms 5 0 5 10 15 20Kms.
Position of Dehradun District in INDIA
Dehradun
a
Position of Dehradun District In UTTAR PRADESH
b
HIMACHAL PRADESH
UTTARKASHI
TEHRI GARHWAL
SAHARANPUR
GARHWAL
BIJNOR
TUNI
CHAKRATA
KALSI
VIKASNAGAR
MUSSOORIE
SAHASPUR
DEHRADUN
RAIPUR
DOIWALA
RISHIKESH
TONS R.
YAMUNA R.
Asan R.
To Saharanpur
To Hardwar
To Narendra-nagar
31° 0′
45′
30′
15′
30° 0′
77° 45′
78° 0′
78° 15′
© GOVERNMENT OF INDIA COPYRIGHT 1990

FIG. 10.1

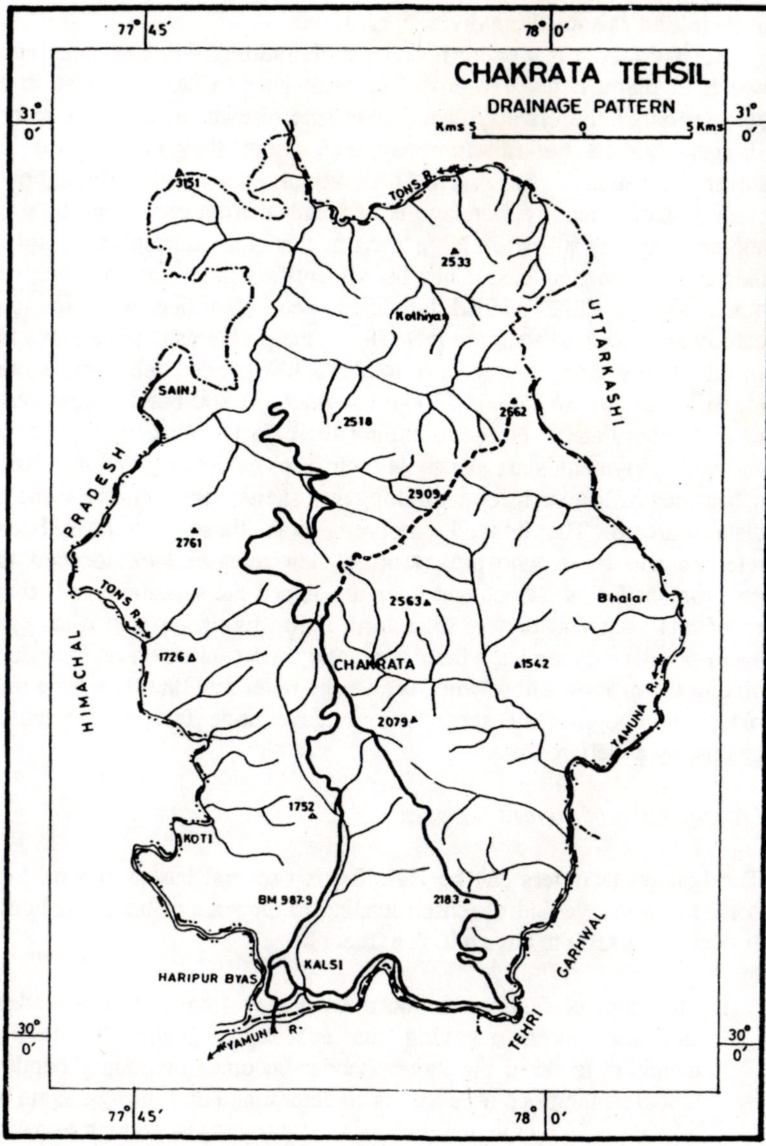

77° 45′
78° 0′
CHAKRATA TEHSIL
DRAINAGE PATTERN
Kms 5 0 5 Kms
31° 0′
30° 0′
3151
TONS R.
2533
Kolhiyan
UTTARKASHI
SAINJ
2518
2662
2909
HIMACHAL PRADESH
2761
TONS R.
2563
Bhalar
1726
CHAKRATA
1542
YAMUNA R.
2079
1752
KOTI
BM 987·9
2183
GARHWAL
KALSI
HARIPUR BYAS
TEHRI
YAMUNA R.

FIG. 10.2

has been that the common folk of Jaunsar Babar consider exploitation of their kind as something divinely ordained.

Bonded labour is a major form of exploitation in Jaunsar Babar and which in many cases have roots in rural indebtedness as in several other parts of the country. And as is true elsewhere, once the poor villagers borrow but fail to repay their debts, they are chained in slavery through successive generations: seemingly throughout eternity. Consequently, bondage is bequeathed from one generation to another and it is still so in large parts of this beautiful region. Despite the fact that bonded labour has been identified from time to time, so much so that 2652 bonded labourers were identified in Dehradun district according to a survey in 1978-79, the problems is too serious to admit of any easy solution. A total 13,300 bonded labourers were identified in Garhwal till 1987, out of which, 11,800 bonded labourers were "rehabilitated". Notwithstanding these facts, ravages of poverty and unemployment, stare starkly at their faces even today and the basic necessities of life such food, clothing and shelter still continue to be a distant dream. The bonded labourers (both those who have been released and those who are awaiting their release) look forward to government for assistance and have developed the syndrome of taking relief and compensation as their birth-right, giving birth to a strange socio-political dynamics which is creating discrimination and tension among the groups. Those who receive the relief feel that they have not received enough while those who receive none feel discriminated against by a welfare state.

Classification of Bonded Labourer

The bonded labourers can be classified on several bases: of work, of period of bondage and of reason leading to the state of bonded labour. It would be useful to have a look at them here:

(i) The chief of family who borrows money from a money-lender, and attempts at repaying the debt by engaging his family members to serve the money-lender becomes hereditary bonded labourer: the price of labour is so determined that the aggregate of labour put in by the members of the family is just enough to cover the interest accrued on the principal sum borrowed.

(ii) The chief of family (or members) who borrow money from the money-lender for discharging social obligations such as marriage, or for treating ailment or for purchasing the animals, become bonded for a certain period of time but receive in lieu of labour a small sum, which for male labourers is Rs. 8, for the female labourers in Rs. 6, and for children it is a paltry Rs. 5, sums that are deducted from the debt as debt repayment. Mercifully such labourers though bonded are also served meals twice a day howsoever simple that may be.

(iii) The more unfortunate ones due to their economic distress go in for loan from the money-lenders by mortgaging their property and engage their family members for repayment of their debt. The wages payable for labour are deducted from the principal amount borrowed, as debt repayment where the wage rates range from Rs.8 per day for the male to Rs.5 for the child labour. But a large segment of these people can never get rid of the burden of debt because no sooner is their earlier debt repaid, that they run into fresh debts and the process continues cumulatively and consecutively.

Characteristics of Bonded Labour

The characteristics of bonded labour are varied. For instance the Tribal Project Authority has found out some harijan groups (*Koltas*) serving as slaves to a village or village Subha. The people belonging to certain castes such as *bajgi*, blacksmith, trumpet players and *dhaki* are afflicted with same system. Though, most of bonded labourers are from harijan families, (approximately 80%) yet, some poor people belonging to higher castes have been sucked into the system of bonded labourers. Only males are made bonded labourers. Generally, males between 18 to 50 years of age are engaged as bonded labourers. Women go in for outdoor work in the absence of their men only. A 50 year old bonded labourer would in all probability be a hereditary bonded labourer.

The number of hereditary bonded labourers now has reduced considerably, but the number of the people engaged as bonded labourers for a certain fixed period is on the increase. The people working as bonded labourers do not disclose the name of their employer both out of fear of reprobation in the hands of their "masters" and out of a sense of security they have out of the arrangement and equilibrium achieved, howsoever, inequitious it may appear to outsiders.

ERGOGRAPH

Daily routine of Bonded Labourer

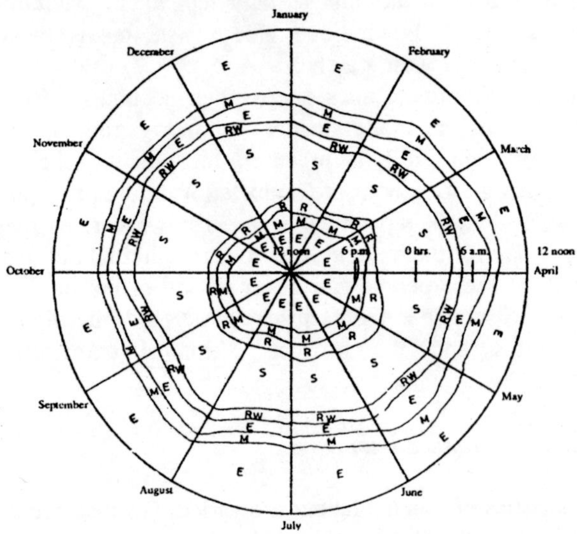

Index

E	Economic activities
R	Recreation
M	Meal
S	Sleeping
RW	Routine work

FIG. 10.3

Index

E = Economic activities; R = Recreation; M = Meal; S = Sleeping; RW = Routine work

The manner in which a typical bonded labour is exploited is best shown with the help Fig. 10.3. The centre of the circle depicts 12 noon of a day and any point on the circumference shows 12 noon of the following day. It is clear that the typical day of a bonded labour consists of economic activities recreation, boarding, sleeping and daily chores, like that of any other human being, but the differences are:

(a) that economic activities are confined to serving the master;
(b) that recreation is usually restricted to gossiping and
(c) that the hours of working for the master varies according as the amount of sunlight available during the month under reference and therefore on the face of it is exploitative.

A few more comments about the last characteristic would be in order. It is apparent from the ergograph that economic activity is on the rise from April onwards till August, and then economic activity is at the minimum during the months of December and January. One would have expected that the hours of work would vary with the season, that is, during cultivation and harvesting seasons the bonded labourers would be required to work more, and during lean season they would be required to work less. But that is not the case usually, which reinforces the intuitive finding that the bonded labourers are not necessarily engaged in agricultural activities though during the cultivation and harvesting seasons they are put to serving the agricultural sector as well.

In a region so devastatingly characterised by bonded labour, it is natural that children of bonded labourers are deprived of education either due to debt or due to hereditary bonded labourership or some combination of the two. The children of bonded labourers conceive that they are born only to serve the landlord's family: they rear cattle and feel satisfied because for them education is futile. However, of late, they have started taking education with some degree of seriousness, up to primary level, but only with regard to the male children: the female children are deprived of education through and through, and though this social discrimination between the male and the female child is lessening gradually, a lot remains to be done.

Housing : The Style of Living

The uniqueness of the habitation of the people of Jaunsar-Babar is best reflected in their homestead: they are both interesting and at once intriquing. Usually one homestead consists of two units as shown in Fig. 10.4. One unit in the living unit and the-second unit is a store. It would be worth our while having a look at the two units rather closely.

Living Unit

Let us look at the living unit first. It is usually a double-storeyed house or more precisely "one and a half storeyed" dwelling. The ground floor is usually 6 feet in height and the first floor has a height of about ten feet, with walls made out of stone blocks and muds and having wooden sleepers inbetween. The roofs are made either out of slate slabs or wooden blocks cut out of the forest to which the people have free access.

The access to the two floors are independent of each other. Doors (one on either sides) giving access to the ground floor are usually 2 to 3 feet in height. A wooden flight of ladder leads the inhabitants from the ground to the first floor doorway, which again is 2-3 feet in height. There is a balcony encircling the entire first floor, and there is second door to the first floor that can be reached by walking along the balcony.

The ground floor is for animals and the first floor is for human habitation. The ground floor is divided into two parts, with one part kept separate for goats and sheeps, and the other the exclusive preserve of the cattle and buffaloes. The first floor is also divided into two parts. As one is lead by the flight of ladder one steps to the low (2-3 feet high) doorway from the ground, to the first floor, one gets into a small corridor dividing the first floor into two parts on either side. On one side are two bed rooms, and on the other are the kitchen and grain store. The outer sleeping room, that is the room nearer to the entry, is for the inmates of the house with an almirah only and the inner bed room is for the guests, having an almirah and a box both. There is usually a passage from the inmates bed rooms to the basement. There are one or two small windows for ventilation on each floor of the dwelling unit.

Store Unit

The store unit is situated a few paces away from the living unit. Like the living unit, the store unit is also "one and a half storeyed", with several differences:

HOUSE TYPE OF JAUNSAR BABAR TRIBES

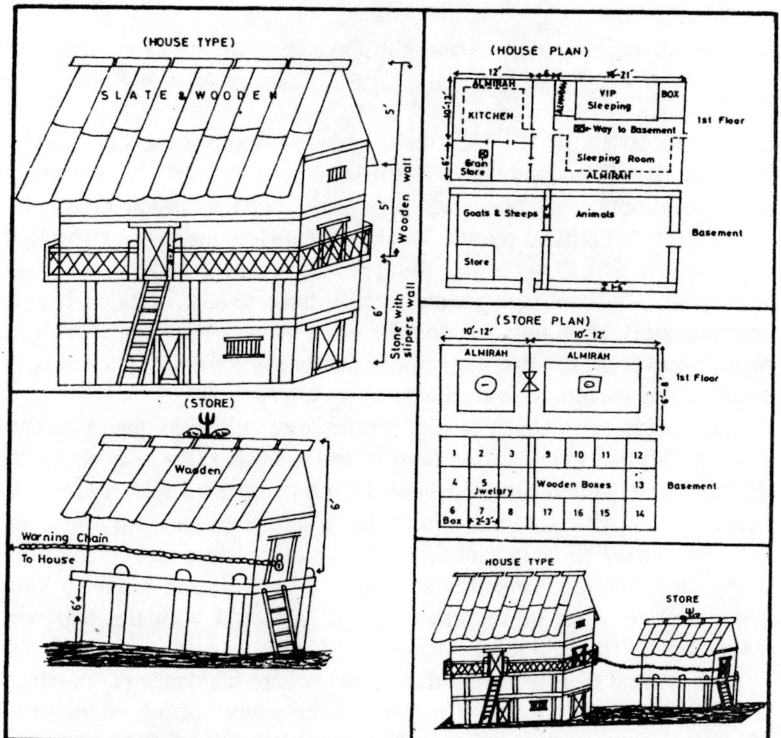

FIG. 10.4

One, there is no access to the basement from the ground level;
Two, while the ground floor is 6 feet (or nearly so) in height, the first floor is of 6 fect also (unlike 10 feet in the living unit) in height;
Three, there is no balcony around the first floor;
Four, there is only one access to the first floor through again a low doorway (of 2 to 3 feet height) which can be reached (again) directly from the ground; and
Five, there is no other opening in the store unit, not even windows, whatever the dimension.

The access to the basement or the ground floor, of the store unit is from the first floor internally. The first floor is divided into two parts (both interconnected) one after the other, and the basement can be accessed from both the rooms. The basement (like the two consecutive rooms of the first floor) is also divided into two parts but are not inter-connected. The basement rooms usually have several wooden boxes, approximately 16 in number, and the room in the basement, which can be accessed from the first floor room that is away from the doorway is usually used to store the valuables and jewellery.

The locking and alarm system for the store unit is unique in several respects. The door on the first floor of the store unit (the only access to the store unit) which can be accessed from the ground with a ladder is bolted from outside and has a fairly large sized bell securedly fastened to it. From the bell is a chain that leads up to the sleeping rooms of the living unit. The mechanism is so designed that as soon as the locking system of the door of the store unit is tampered with the bell will automatically ring and raise alarm.

It is natural that the social framework where incidence of bondage is high and where education is limited, the people of are engulfed in old evils, outmoded customs and superstitions whether it relates to marriage, festivals and other socio-religious practices. The tribal people of Jaunsar Babar deem all spheres of life as being related with deities, to please whom prayers are offered in the temples of every village and different fairs are organised at different times. In particular, *Mahashu* deity is worshipped thrice a day all over Jaunsar Babar, and the beating of drums is the indication of call for the prayers. Supper or dinner or evening meals are not taken till the drum is beaten, heard and responded to.

The Institution of Marriage

Child marriage has been a characteristic feature of Jaunsar Babar and babies in arm being married away among some harijans is not uncommon even today, and simultaneously, polyandry and polygamy prevail. The institution of marriage is considered by the people of Jaunsar Babar as both sacred and divinely ordained, and a social institution. Several forms of marriage are found which can be classified as under:

(a) polyandry
(b) polygamy
(c) polyandry - polygamy
(d) polygamy - polyandry

Whereas the phenomena of polyandry and polygamy are usually straight-forward, the other two varieties are somewhat more complex, and whereas the phenomena of polyandry and polygamy are area specific, the other two varieties are not. And while the former two admit of economic explanations, the latter two admit of a more involved rationalisation.

Polyandry is more pronounced in the Jaunsar area, but polygamy is more distinct in Babar area. In Jaunsar area we met two villagers Shri Surendra Singh and Kirti Singh of village Chhajar Hartar (See Fig. 10.6). Surendra Singh and Kirti Singh's mother was Puran Devi who was married to Mazer Singh and Shrichand Singh (who were also two brothers). The two brothers Surendra Singh and Kirti Singh also have a common wife, named Meena Devi. They explained that in Jaunsar area the availability of land was limited (high scarcity element) and yield on land was concurrently low. Hence by resorting to polyandry the pressure on land was contained and the density of population kept under some leash.

In case of Babar region, however, polygamy was the dominant strand in the institution of marriage. We met Sri Nepal Singh Chauhan who had three wives. It was explained that Babar area had a relatively high yield on land and the availability of labour as variable input (to be combined with fixed factor, land) was rather limited. Polygamy is believed to be more conducive to a higher rate in population growth and hence encouraged, so that the imbalance in man-land ratio is corrected.

Village : Birnard Bastil

POLYANDRY

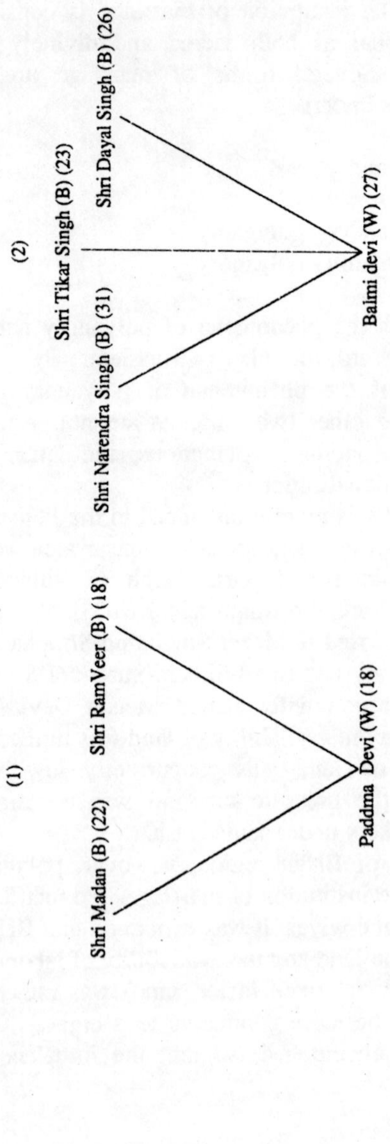

FIG. 10.5

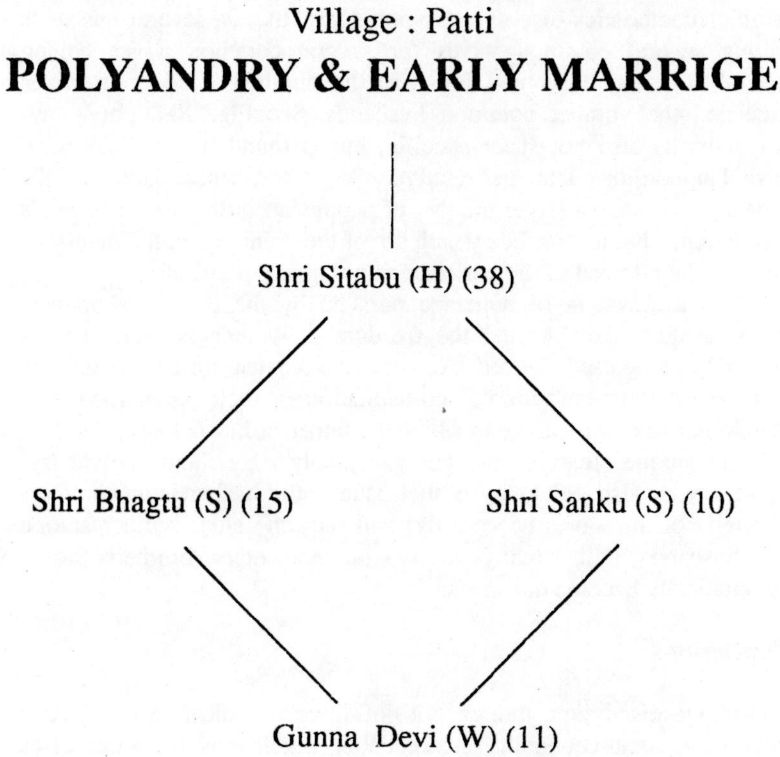

FIG. 10.6

The phenomenon of polyandry-polygamy is somewhat more involved and does not exhibit any spatial bias. In polyandry-polygamy, there are several husbands having several common wives, or put in another way, several wives have several common husbands, and where the number of common husbands exceed the number of common wives. See Fig. 10.7 for instance in village Penwa we met Shri Kishan Singh, Shri Kedar Singh and Shri Madan Singh, who have two common wives, Roopa Devi and Jabbo Devi. Generally, polyandry-polygamy was rationalised in families which are keen to prevent fragmentation of landholdings, that is, in families which believed that to prevent deterioration in man-land ratio, it was necessary to have lesser number of children than perhaps would be permissible under polygamy *per se*.

The other variety of marriage, namely, polygamy-polyandry has the same characteristics of polyandry-polygamy, that is, several husbands having several common wives (or several common wives having several common husbands) but here the number of common wives exceeded the number common husbands. See Fig. 10.8 polygamy-polyandry is also not space-specific, but is found in families which have landholdings that are relatively large and where land has the capacity to sustain a larger number of people, according to the people's perception. That is, families which are of the opinion that the man-land ratio can be allowed to rise, resorted to polygamy-polyandry.

Thus the system of marriage pursued by the people of Jaunsar Babar is quite flexible and the freedom to women is more than is generally recognised. Indeed like men, the women are free to indulge in premarital or extra-marital co-habitation in their parents' village, though not so in the village to which the father-in-law belongs.

An unique feature of polygamy-polyandry, and polyandry-polygamy as also polygamy is that usually the husbands are brothers (though not the wives necessarily) and only the elder brother among the husbands will ritually marry, but the other brothers would automatically become husbands.

Conclusions

The above discussion, though not definitive is indicative of several interesting socio-economic phenomenon, which may be summarised briefly as under:

(a) Bondage is a way of life for the poorer people and is in practice in all forms.
(b) The dominance of religion-superstition, as in all under-developed societies, is quite marked.
(c) The people value their animal wealth more than their alternative movable assets, which is why animals are housed in their living units and not in the store unit of their habitats.
(d) The hospitality of the simple village folk is proverbial.
(e) Marriage is looked upon both as an institution than a divinely ordained mandate, and therefore, marriage is by and large regulated having regard to the land, its quality and quantity both taken care of. To that extent the people are rational, given the socio-economic framework and state of art and education.

Village:- Penwa

POLYANDRY-POLYGAMY

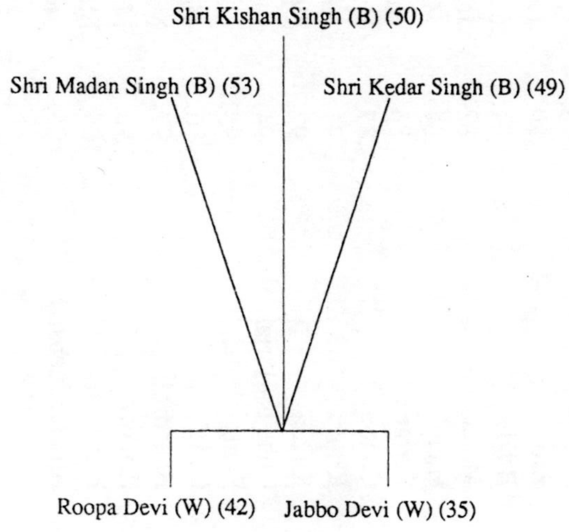

FIG. 10.7

POLYGAMY-POLYANDRY

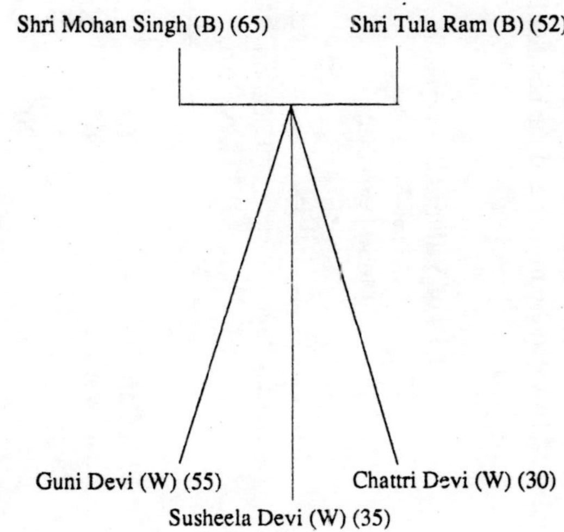

FIG. 10.8

(f) If the institution of bonded labour is sought to be abolished, it is essential to take into account the security net that has been established between the master and the bonded labour.

List of Villages Surveyed

Chakrata Tehsil

(District Dehra Dun)

Location Code No.	Name of Vilage	Location Code No.	Name of Vilage
3.	Bhat Garhi	62.	Kunuwa
5.	Bhagawat	65.	Kandoi
7.	Raigi	66.	Bayala
9.	Dersa	70.	Undawa
13.	Raru	71.	Asoi
15.	Sainj	74.	Koti
17.	Hatal	77.	Masak
18.	Birnadbastil	78.	Buraila
19.	Kuna	80.	Lohari
20.	Bagi	81.	Seejla
21.	Maindrath	82.	Jadi
22.	Hanol	84.	Matiyana
23.	Purtar	86.	Bassau
24.	Chatra	87.	Haja
26.	Koti	91.	Bhoopau
28.	Kanda	92.	Gawela
36.	Chhajar Hartar	94.	Kota
43.	Sunir	95.	Gamari
47.	Chjoi	96.	Meloth
49.	Bhandroli	97.	Manjhgaon
51.	Penuwa	98.	Malaitha
53.	Kunain	105.	Mohana
54.	Amarar Jhabarar	106.	Sujau

Contd.

Location Code No.	Name of Vilage	Location Code No.	Name of Vilage
111.	Kharsi	185.	Phatio
112.	Kandidhar	186.	Echhla
113.	Punaha Pokhari	190.	Samalta Dadauli
115.	Thanta	191.	Kakari
116.	Jogiyou	192.	Kanbaua
125.	Buraswa	193.	Sakni
126.	Pati	194.	Alsi
127.	Rawana	195.	Malaitha
131.	Sahiya	201.	Badanu
135.	Rampur Sharana	202.	Datnu
138.	Derio	203.	Gothan Joshi
140.	Nada	204.	Hamrau
141.	Lawari	207.	Kothi
142.	Chatar Chhauntar	209.	Hoda
143.	Kandoi	210.	Magrauli
145.	Lakha Mandal	211.	Dakeṛana
149.	Kandichama Gata	214.	Koruwa
150.	Kunna	219.	Nithala
153.	Chhatau	221.	Rikhar
154.	Chor Kunawa	222.	Bisoi
162.	[illegible]adola	227.	Salga
167.	Nagau	228.	Naraya
169.	Makhti	238.	Teepau
174.	Rani	248.	Bhanjhra
175.	Bantau	255.	Lailta
178.	Udpalta	257.	Desau
180.	Naivi	259.	Danda
181.	Bori	263.	Nichhiya
182.	Khatasa	267.	Bhugtari
183.	Jhusau Bhakrau	285.	Thaina
184.	Pata	289.	Kothi Bharondi

Contd.

Location Code No.	Name of Vilage	Location Code No.	Name of Vilage
297.	Biyasbhud	326.	Khunna Alman
298.	Haripur	327.	Ludhera
299.	Basan	328.	Sariyana
302.	Jendo	329.	Chila
307.	Asta	331.	Lohari
310.	Mundhan	332.	Loharna
311.	Rampur	333.	Munsi
312.	Gadol	334.	Laksiyar
320.	Dweena	335.	Dhiroi
321.	Silla	336.	Khadi
322.	Lachha	356.	Luhari
323.	Bisoi	357.	Lakwar

INDEX